HUGGING PORCUPINES

Also by Mike Anderson

Rekindle Your Professional Fire: Powerful Habits for Becoming a More Well-Balanced Teacher

———————————

Tackling the Motivation Crisis: How to Activate Student Learning Without Behavior Charts, Pizza Parties, or Other Hard-to-Quit Incentive Systems

———————————

What We Say and How We Say It Matter: Teacher Talk That Improves Student Learning and Behavior

———————————

Learning to Choose, Choosing to Learn: The Key to Student Motivation and Achievement

———————————

The Well-Balanced Teacher: How to Work Smarter and Stay Sane Inside the Classroom and Out

———————————

Teacher Talk That Matters (Quick Reference Guide)

MIKE ANDERSON

HUGGING PORCUPINES

MONTH-BY-MONTH STRATEGIES TO SUPPORT OUR MOST CHALLENGING STUDENTS

iste+ascd

Arlington, Virginia USA

iste+ascd™

2111 Wilson Boulevard, Suite 300 • Arlington, VA 22201 USA
Phone: 800-933-2723 or 703-578-9600
Website: iste-ascd.org • Email: memsupport@iste-ascd.org
Author guidelines: ascd.org/write

Richard Culatta, *Chief Executive Officer;* Genny Ostertag, *Managing Director, Book Acquisitions & Editing;* Mary Beth Nielsen, *Director, Book Editing & Design;* Liz Wegner, *Senior Editor;* Donald Ely for Three Ring Studio, *Graphic Designer;* Circle Graphics, *Typesetter;* Emily Reed, *Senior Director, Publishing Operations*; Christopher Logan, *Senior Production Specialist;* Shajuan Martin, *E-Publishing Specialist*

All links in this book are correct as of the publication date below but may have become inactive or otherwise modified since that time. If you notice a broken link, email books@ascd.org; include "Link Update" in the subject line; and in the message, specify the link, the book title, and the page number on which the link appears.

PAPERBACK ISBN: 978-1-4166-3447-8 Product #126020 n5/26
PDF EBOOK ISBN: 978-1-4166-3448-5; see Books in Print for other formats.
Quantity discounts are available: email programteam@ascd.org or call 800-933-2723, ext. 5773, or 703-575-5773. For desk copies, go to ascd.org/deskcopy.

Library of Congress Cataloging-in-Publication Data is available.
Library of Congress Control Number: 2026000287

---

35 34 33 32 31 30 29 28 27 26   1 2 3 4 5 6 7 8 9 10 11 12

HUGGING PORCUPINES

PART I

Who Are Our Porcupines?

Who Are Our Porcupines?

James arrived in my 5th grade class one morning in early October. I knew I was getting a new student, but I had been told he would arrive in about a week, so I was surprised when he sauntered into my classroom just before other students arrived. He was tall and walked with a wide stance, feet turned slightly out and shoulders back. His head swiveled from side to side as he eyed the room incredulously. "Dude!" he bellowed. "This room is weird!"

I offered my hand. "Hi. You must be James. I'm Mr. Anderson."

To be fair, my classroom *was* a bit weird. A circle of chairs was set up for morning meeting, which would begin as soon as students were settled. Tables were arranged around the room so that students could work together but were spaced out enough so they wouldn't be on top of each other. A couch, donated by a family the previous year, was a perfect spot to read a book or work on some math problems with a friend. A loft flanked one side of the room. It offered a different (and fun!) workspace while also blocking the hallway that ran through our classroom—a vestige of the school's failed attempt at the open-classroom concept of the 1970s. A few tropical plants and lamps gave the room a homey feel. Under the loft was a terrarium for our classroom's pet king snake.

James was joining us from a classroom where students were lined up in rows, sitting in alphabetical order. He was used to a teacher's desk at the front of the room (I didn't have one) and rigid desk-chairs joined by the metal bar that I remember (and hated) from high school.

So his reaction to his new classroom, though a bit abrasive, was understandable. It *was* weird. His reaction became even more understandable when his father, James Sr., later told me the story of why they had moved across the country. James Jr.'s parents had just split up. His mother met someone online and announced that she was leaving. She had also stated, in front of James Jr., that she couldn't take James Jr. and his behaviors anymore and that he was part of the reason she was leaving. James Sr., not knowing what else to do, drove James Jr. and a few of their belongings across the country in his pickup truck and moved in with his mom. James Sr. told me this story as he sobbed about hitting rock bottom and losing his soulmate. I remember handing him tissue after tissue as we talked for about 45 minutes.

Unsurprisingly, James Jr. was a disaster in class. I gave him plenty of time to warm up to our classroom and the other students, letting him simply observe morning meetings until he felt ready to join. The first few days, he sat with eyes wide and arms folded protectively across his chest as students greeted each other, played fun academic games, and shared personal stories with each other. I had a few other students help James learn the routines of the room, and I spent extra time with him in each academic subject, attempting to get a sense of his academic skills and interests.

Even with this gentle guidance and support, James was exhausting. He would holler at me from across the room, "Mr. Anderson! My pencil just broke! I need another pencil!" He was sitting right near the pencil sharpener and the class supply bin of pencils. We were in the middle of a science/writing unit where we would head outside each day to write about and sketch plants and animals that we saw at the edge of our school's playground. James was terrified of writing (he was incredibly low in every academic subject), so he faked asthma attacks when we were heading outside: "Mr. Anderson! (Gasp!) I can't (Gasp!) breathe! I need to (Gasp!) go to the nurse! (Gasp!)"

Yet he was also so lovable. He could be so kind and sweet when he wasn't freaking out about something. He clearly wanted to make friends, but he didn't know how. He was funny. (And, by the way, you can't be funny without being smart.) His exaggerated facial expressions and timing when delivering a funny line were impeccable. I remember wishing I could just hang out with him and play Monopoly all day—he'd be a blast. Trying to get him engaged in math and reading was another story. He could be maddeningly defiant and shut down so quickly. He was so skilled at self-sabotage.

The most dramatic episode with James came several weeks into his tenure in our classroom. We were taking a field trip to hike a small local mountain as part of our culmination of our writing/science unit exploring local ecosystems. I just couldn't take him with us. He was too dysregulated, and I worried that he would shut down the field trip for everyone with a meltdown on the trail. I called his father and let him know that I had a colleague who would take James in his class for the day, and that we were setting him up to have a great day. I also emphasized how important it was for James to come to school. I didn't want him to get the impression that dysregulated and outrageous behavior would result in him staying home.

The morning of the field trip rolled around. I was in my classroom, making final preparations, when James Sr. walked in, looking sheepish. He muttered, "James isn't feeling well this morning and needs to stay home sick. Could you give me his work so he can do it at home?" My heart sank, but I didn't have the time or energy to fight this battle in the moment. Students would arrive in less than 30 minutes. I was sitting with James Sr., going over some things James Jr. could do during the day, when guess who walked into the room—clearly not sick? "Come on, Dad! What's takin' you so long?"

James Sr. got visibly upset and pointed his finger at James Jr. "I told you to wait in the truck! You get back out there!" James Jr. rolled his eyes dramatically and ambled back out of the classroom.

A couple of minutes later, I was finished explaining the work to James's dad when a voice crackled on the intercom. "Mr. Anderson. There's a boy in the office crying and asking for you." I walked briskly down to the office to find James Jr., shaken and upset.

Apparently, while he was waiting in his dad's truck, he noticed that it wasn't parked squarely in the space, so he decided to fix it. The keys were in the truck, so he slid into the driver's seat, turned on the ignition, put the truck in reverse, and smashed into another car.

When James Jr. heard that the principal was calling the police to report the car accident, he thought he was going to jail. Amid this chaos, James Sr. appeared in the office. He heard what happened and bellowed at James Jr.: "That's it! I can't take it anymore! I'm sending you back to your mother!" So first his mom abandoned him, and now his dad was giving up on him. Ouch.

James struggled a lot that year, but he also made some real progress. As he learned to trust me and the other students, he let his guard down and started to accept more help. His academic skills were still lagging at the end of the year, but he made real growth. He continued to need an individualized behavior plan throughout the year, but he spent more time in the classroom and needed fewer trips to the counseling room to calm down.

James finished the school year with us, and it was tough to see him leave for the summer. He could still be a handful, but he had come so far.

I saw him three years later when our class had a reunion. We gathered one afternoon in the spring of that class's 8th grade year to reconnect and open the time capsule we'd put together in 5th grade. James attended, and he seemed to be doing well. He was playing football and doing fine in school. He was calm and relaxed.

Through the years, James was someone I often thought about. He would pop into my head at random times, and I'd wonder, "How's that kid doing?" Years later, he reached out, and we corresponded a few times via email. You'll hear about this at the end of the book.

Who Are Our Porcupines?

If you've worked with students for any significant amount of time, you've likely worked with kids like James. Throughout the course of my career, I've had many. We think about them while commuting to and from school (and often on weekends and when we're trying to sleep at night). They're often hard to engage and disruptive. They can be prickly—pushing us away as we try to get close. Or they might be quiet and withdrawn, hiding in the back of the room or covering their head with their hoods. They melt down easily, dissolving into tears or exploding in rage, seemingly out of nowhere. Yet they can also be sweet, kind, and caring. Every now and then, their defenses drop, and we see their potential. Halley, normally bristly and angry, laughs as she plays a math game with Molly. Jared, usually stoic and cold, cracks a smile at a dumb joke we drop. We bring our class to work with a group of younger students, and suddenly Susan, who usually won't cooperate with anyone, becomes a patient and empathetic tutor as she reads with a young student.

How do kids end up in this place? How do they become porcupines? There's no one profile or description that fits them all, but there are a few common reasons why kids can be prickly in school.

Trauma

A former student of mine lived on the edge of fight, flight, or freeze nearly all the time. If someone walked by our classroom, his head would pop up to see who it was, his eyes alert and wary. I'd say, "Hey, Allen" to ask him how his poetry was coming along, and he'd explode, "I wasn't doin' nothin'! You're always picking on me!" It was almost impossible for him to focus on any academic task because his radar was always on high alert, assessing every-thing around him as a possible threat. Once I learned about his background, I understood what was going on. He was pushed out of a moving car by his mother when he was 4 years old. By the time I had him in 5th grade, he had never lived with any one adult for more than 10 months at a time. His mother was in and out of jail for drug use and dealing. And this was only the small part of his story that I knew. We all suspected that this was the tip of the iceberg.

Trauma has significant impacts on children's brain function and development. "Stress and trauma can adversely affect the ability to make decisions, solve problems, and set goals" (Budge & Parrett, 2018, p. 39). Adverse childhood experiences (ACEs) such as substance abuse in the home, witnessing or experiencing domestic violence, and parental divorce (to name just a few) can have a profound impact on children's brain development. "In the midst of extreme stress, our bodies are forced to respond via a heightened state of alert known as the *fight, flight, or freeze response.* Our bodies were designed to be in that state only for brief periods and only in the face of extreme danger. But when children are exposed to acute trauma, the brain shifts its operation from development to stress response, which can have lasting repercussions" (Souers & Hall, 2016, p. 21).

Allen's outbursts weren't his fault. Just like kids who hide under desks or run away from school when overwhelmed, Allen was reacting the only way he knew how—the way his brain was programmed to respond. Erikah Messamer, a paraprofessional in Manchester, New Hampshire, describes students who are experiencing ACEs as "kids navigating adult situations and solving them with childlike solutions" (personal communication, October 11, 2024).

Let's also not forget the impacts of living in poverty. Although poverty isn't itself a trauma, it often leads to instability and a lack of basic needs being met, which can be traumatic. I've had students living in homeless shelters and in campgrounds who came to school hungry, dirty, and exhausted each morning. When students' most basic needs aren't being met—when their brains are spending almost all their energy on surviving—there's not much energy left for fractions, essays, or social studies projects.

Neurodivergence

My son has ADHD, and school was often tough. He's really smart and incredibly self-motivated, but sitting still to study for a test (that he didn't really care about) or writing an essay (that he wasn't really interested in) or filling out a physics worksheet (that he thought was pointless) was torture. He struggled to hold himself together all day and would be exhausted when he got home.

ADHD is just one of many ways our students might be neurodivergent. Autism, Tourette syndrome, processing disorder, oppositional defiance disorder (ODD), and Down syndrome are just a few others. Some students might have other learning disabilities such as dyslexia, dysgraphia, and dyscalculia. Each of these has a unique set of challenges and also gifts that don't fit neatly under one profile. Autism alone has a wide range of variations. But each of them can make school more challenging. It's hard enough for many of us to take direction and have to work on something we don't want to do, but imagine if your brain was wired for hyper self-direction, like people who have ODD or autism. Many of our porcupines have diagnosed or undiagnosed conditions that make school more challenging.

Mental Health Conditions

Jonathan Haidt (2024) makes a convincing argument that anxiety is on the rise in children in the United States and many other parts of the world. The shifting landscape of childhood, where kids spend less time in face-to-face interactions and more time online with social media, has led to a rise in many mental health conditions including anxiety. Let's also not forget that the whole world endured a trauma as we struggled through the COVID pandemic, which led many to feel increased anxiety and isolation.

Anxiety is just one of many mental health conditions we may see in our students. In my time in the classroom, I had students who were diagnosed with depression and obsessive-compulsive disorder. One student was seeing a therapist to manage panic attacks. Another was exhibiting symptoms of bipolar disorder and schizophrenia in 4th grade. His mother was told by doctors that age 9 was a bit early to officially diagnose those disorders, but he was headed in that direction. (She was already diagnosed with both.) Again, some of our porcupines may have a diagnosed or undiagnosed mental health disorder that makes interacting with peers or teachers or engaging in active and interactive learning more challenging.

Skills and Strategies That Don't Match Expectations

Not surprisingly, many kids who struggle with learning to read and write, or who struggle with number sense and other basic math skills, also struggle with behavior. It's hard to stay positively engaged in schoolwork if you're always feeling incompetent. There are other skills kids might struggle with. They might have a hard time with key social skills such as cooperation, compromise, taking turns, listening to others, or perspective taking. Or they might struggle with regulation skills such as self-control, managing impulsivity, understanding their emotions, perseverance, flexibility, or frustration tolerance.

Students might struggle with these skills for a variety of reasons. They might not have seen other people demonstrate these skills. They may never have been taught how to do these things or been given a chance to practice. They may have even developed some coping skills that work at home but aren't considered appropriate at school. Kids might hide under furniture at home to stay safe when adults get violent. Or they may have to yell and scream to be noticed or have their needs met in a chaotic home. When viewed this way, these aren't really misbehaviors. They're strategies that don't match school expectations.

Too often in schools, kids who struggle with key skills—whether they're traditional academic ones (such as reading comprehension or writing fluency) or ones involving self-management or working with others—receive punitive feedback and consequences (poor grades and punishments) instead of supportive skill building. This all has a compounding effect. We shouldn't be surprised when some porcupines get more defensive and bristly the more they experience failure, shame, and humiliation in schools. It's one reason that middle and high school porcupines can be so much harder to work with the older they get.

Any one of these conditions can make navigating school incredibly challenging for some students, but let's not forget that some kids have multiple challenges. They may be experiencing trauma *and* have a learning disability. They may have a mental health condition *and* have not learned key skills needed for success in school. James, who you heard about earlier in this chapter, was going through multiple major life disruptions (his parents getting divorced and moving across the country), hadn't been taught many core academic and behavioral skills needed for school success, and was falling far behind academically. Is it any wonder he was a mess?

I felt for James, but I was also frustrated by him. These can be hard kids to work with. They test our patience and make us feel incompetent. They can say mean things and hurt our feelings. But they're also the ones that make this crazy profession have meaning and purpose. When we break through their defenses and help them learn and grow, we feel a rush of satisfaction. When we bump into one in the grocery store years later, and they light up and want to tell us how they're doing, we remember why we went into teaching in the first place. I'll never forget a scene from when I was student teaching. My cooperating teacher, Nancy Moretta, was an amazing educator who cherished working with the most challenging students in a high-poverty school. I marveled at the humor, patience, and genuine love she poured into her students. One day at dismissal, a young adult walked through the door. He looked like a tough customer—someone who had already lived a hard life. He entered the classroom, and Nancy lit up with a huge smile and ran over to give him a hug. This young man had just been released from prison and was on parole, and one of the first people he wanted to visit was his former 4th grade teacher.

There are plenty of real-life stories of people who struggled in school but survived and went on to lead remarkable lives. Winston Churchill, Temple Grandin, Eddie Murphy, C. S. Lewis, David Lee Roth, Ryan Gosling, Dav Pilkey, Adam Sandler, Gillian Lynne, and Oprah Winfrey (to name just a few) all experienced huge challenges as kids yet went on to accomplish great things. They are a good reminder that neurodivergence, traumatic experiences, or even just stubbornness and mischievousness might present challenges in school, but people can always persevere and find success.

Using This Book

This book offers practical strategies and helpful insights for supporting porcupines so they can be as successful as possible, both in school and later on in life. In the rest of Part I, we'll spend time thinking about why these students struggle so much in school. Porcupines can be mystifying, especially for those of us who breezed through and enjoyed school. We'll consider the following questions: Why do they push us away when we try to get close? Why do they refuse to work on academics when learning is the ticket to a better life later on? Why do they break rules so often? We'll also explore a few of the common strategies and practices we implement with the best of intentions that don't seem to help our most challenging kids.

In Part II, we'll get into the nitty gritty work of how to support our porcupines all year long. This section is organized according to various stages of the school year. You'll learn about simple and powerful practices that you can use throughout the year to support your porcupines.

At one point during the research phase of this book, I explored the profiles and stories of famous people who struggled in school. Something that stood out to me as I read about people who overcame childhood struggles in school was that nearly all of them had at least one trusted adult who supported them and cared about them when they were young. It might have been a parent, a nanny, or a teacher. You can be that person for your porcupines. They desperately need adults who understand them, don't give up on them, and support them, even when they're at their worst.

Let's get started by deepening our understanding of why our porcupines so often struggle. We'll begin with relationships. Why do some of your porcupines struggle so much with connection, and why might they push you away as you try to get close?

Why Do Porcupines Struggle with Relationships?

"If one more administrator tells me to 'just build a positive relationship' with a challenging kid, I'm going to scream!"

Sound familiar? More than one teacher has shared similar sentiments with me over the last few years. There are a couple of problems with this well-intentioned advice. The advice makes it sound like either (a) something the teacher hadn't thought of before or (b) something that's easy to do. Both assumptions miss the mark. Most of us already believe that relationships are important, and we've tried to connect with our toughest kids. But it's hard.

In this chapter, we'll explore the power of relationships in depth. We'll start by checking our assumptions at the door. Are relationships really as important as we think? We'll then dig into what it actually means to build a "positive" teacher–student relationship. We'll also explore why some kids struggle to build relationships when we reach out.

Are Positive Teacher–Student Relationships Really That Important?

Rita Pierson was a lifelong educator and a champion of supporting students who are typically underserved. In her TED talk Every Kid Needs a Champion (which has been viewed more than 17 million times), she asserts that relationships are the key to students' success. She relays an anecdote that may speak to many of us: "A colleague said to me one time, 'They don't pay me to like the kids. They pay me to teach a lesson. The kids should learn it. I should teach it. They should learn it. Case closed.' Well, I said to her, 'You know, kids don't learn from people they don't like'" (2013).

If you also believe in the power of positive relationships in the classroom, you likely cheer at this line. You can probably recount stories of students you've connected with who made great strides because of your relationships with them. You likely had teachers who made a huge difference in your life.

But what about Rita's colleague's contention? I've heard teachers voice similar objections about the idea of relationship building. "I'm their teacher, not their friend" and "Kids need to learn to work with lots of different personality types—we can't all be warm and fuzzy" are not uncommon viewpoints in the teacher's room. What if there's something to this viewpoint? Are positive teacher–student relationships really as important as we think? If so, why are they so important? And what the heck *is* a positive teacher–student relationship, anyway?

As it turns out, there's a whole raft of research that highlights the importance of building positive relationships with all students and especially with porcupines.

John Hattie's meta-analysis work is perhaps the best-known and most widely used research in education. His book, *Visible Learning,* is a meta-analysis of more than 800 meta-analyses from across education that uncovers which practices yield the highest achievement results in schools. In particular, the book detailed a meta-analysis of 119 studies (that included data from more than 350,000 students) about teacher–student relationships. The analysis revealed that positive teacher–student relationships (TSRs) have an effect size of 0.72—one of the strongest practices Hattie came across. This is equivalent to nearly two years' growth in one year's time. It placed 11 out of 138 in influences on student achievement. Hattie (2009) stated: "In classes with person-centered teachers, there is more engagement, more respect of self and others, there are fewer resistant behaviors, there is greater nondirectivity (student initiated and student-regulated activities), and there are higher achievement outcomes" (p. 119).

Another meta-analysis—this one of 99 studies of preK–12 students—found strong evidence for the power of positive TSRs. This analysis found significant gains for students in both school engagement and academic achievement when students have positive relationships with their teachers (Roorda et al., 2011).

These are just two of many examples of the robust literature detailing the importance of building positive teacher–student relationships.

Positive TSRs Are Even More Important for Porcupines

Another meta-analysis highlights specific positive school outcomes that almost seem to scream "This is what our porcupines need!" In a paper (Emslander et al., 2025) detailing a synthesis of over 70 years of research across 26 meta-analyses (which includes data from approximately 2.64 million preK–12 students), the authors detailed significant correlations between positive TSRs and eight important student outcomes:

- Academic achievement.
- Academic emotions.
- Appropriate student behavior.
- Behavior problems.
- Executive functions and self-control.
- Motivation.
- School belonging and engagement.
- Well-being.

Look back at that list again with your porcupines in mind. If you could wave your magic wand and conjure up a few positive outcomes you'd want for your most challenging students, you would probably land on these. Many other studies show strong correlations between positive TSRs and student outcomes for students who struggle in school. The meta-analysis of 99 studies from preK to high school noted that TSRs were more important for children who were academically at risk, in particular for children from disadvantaged economic backgrounds and children with learning difficulties (Roorda et al., 2011). A longitudinal study of children from grades preK–8 highlighted that the negative outcomes of negative TSRs are especially true for children with high levels of behavior problems, particularly boys (Hamre & Pianta, 2001).

A study of TSRs in elementary school showed that there is a protective effect of positive TSRs for children with developmental vulnerabilities. Close TSRs had a significant positive impact on these children. They fared much better than similar students who didn't have a close relationship with a teacher (Baker, 2006). A different study of high school students who had been referred for discipline showed that when these students felt like their teachers were trustworthy, they displayed less defiant behavior (Gregory & Ripski, 2008).

Other studies have found that positive TSRs may be especially important for students who are at a higher risk of failing in school due to family background factors (Burchinal et al., 2002; Gruman et al., 2008), academic or behavioral problems (Baker, 2006; Buyse et al., 2008), and special needs such as autism spectrum disorder and speech and language concerns (Di Lisio et al., 2025).

Why Are Positive Relationships So Hard to Build with Some Students?

Porcupines are the students who most need positive TSRs, yet they can be hard to get close to. Why?

Some kids have learned not to trust adults. They may have been hurt by adults outside school, or they may have had negative relationships with adults in school. In an important reminder for all of us, author and educator Jeffrey Benson says that for some students, "adults have been like mountain trolls: unpredictable, dangerous, powerful creatures that walk through their lives, seemingly incapable of listening and unable to recognize human emotions" (2015). They may be understandably reluctant to take the emotional risks needed to get close with us.

Some students may also lack some of the key interpersonal skills or emotional regulation skills needed to interact effectively. They may not have learned how to show empathy or social interest, take others' perspectives, or resolve conflicts without fighting. They may not know how to make appropriate eye contact, use a kind tone of voice, or calm themselves down when they're first getting upset. Some schools have reported to me that more and more children seem to be lacking these foundational skills when they enter school. More than one principal has described some of their kindergartners as "feral" at the beginning of the year. One principal shared a story with me about parents who said that they couldn't even take their kids to the grocery store because their behavior was so out of control, yet they entered kindergarten being expected to sit in a circle and listen to their teacher and peers.

Sometimes we're the ones who struggle to warm up to our students. Some children may be hard to like. This is rarely talked about in education, but I think it's important to acknowledge. It's hard to be physically close to kids who come to school dirty and disheveled or who pick their nose or are sick a lot. It's hard to be emotionally close to kids who cry, scream, or insult others on a regular basis. We may have had previous traumatic experiences with other kids that makes it harder for us to be emotionally vulnerable with our students.

But let's remember that our most challenging kids are also our most vulnerable ones. They're the ones who need us the most.

What Exactly Is a Positive Teacher–Student Relationship?

Supreme Court Justice Potter Stewart once famously refused to define obscenity but said, "I know it when I see it." You might feel the same way about positive teacher–student relationships. You have a vague notion of what one looks and feels like. You know it when you see it. We need to do better than this. (Justice Potter probably should have as well.) It's too subjective. We could all come up with various definitions and criteria of positive teacher–student relationships. In some ways, that's not a bad thing. After all, each relationship will be a bit different, and we might need to connect with different students in different ways. With one student, a bit of gentle joking will bring us closer, while another student may need to connect around a shared interest of sports or movies. Yet as I was reviewing research and literature about positive teacher–student relationships, there were a few key components that kept coming up, and they're a helpful foundation for relationship building with students.

There appear to be two sets of interrelated characteristics that lead to positive teacher–student relationships.

Strategies That Are Warm and Demanding

Positive teacher–student relationships are characterized by teachers who use strategies that are both warm and demanding. These might sound like conflicting ideas, but they're actually complementary.

- **Warm.** We can get to know students beyond their academic work and talk with them about their interests. We can be culturally aware and responsive, showing interest and respect for students' families and backgrounds. We can offer unconditional kindness and friendliness and do lots of "little" things (that aren't so little) like smiling, using students' names, cracking little jokes, and making eye contact. We can show students that we like them and value who they are, creating a climate of friendliness and trust.

- **Demanding.** In addition to being warm, we can also use strategies that are demanding. We should have high expectations and demand a climate of mutual respect. We can hold kids accountable for good behavior but do so through respectful consequences, not harsh punishments. We can be fair and use firm, clear, and nonnegotiable language. This clarity reduces conflict and power struggles. When students are struggling with ongoing challenges, we can work with them collaboratively to help find solutions.

The important balance of these characteristics has been recognized for quite a while. Educator Judith Kleinfeld first coined the term *warm demander* in 1975 to describe teachers who were successful working with indigenous children in Alaska. The key is to be both. If we're warm but not demanding, we slide into permissiveness. We fail to set clear limits and give too many second (and third and fourth . . .) chances. Kids feel unsafe when limits aren't enforced, which can lead to increased dysregulation and limit testing. On the other hand, if we're firm but cold, we become overly authoritarian. Kids fail to connect with us personally and are fearful and resentful as consequences feel harsh and devoid of empathy. This can lead kids to seek revenge and rebel, again increasing dysregulation in the classroom. The sweet spot is somewhere between permissiveness and authoritarianism (Figure 2.1).

FIGURE 2.1
Warm and Demanding

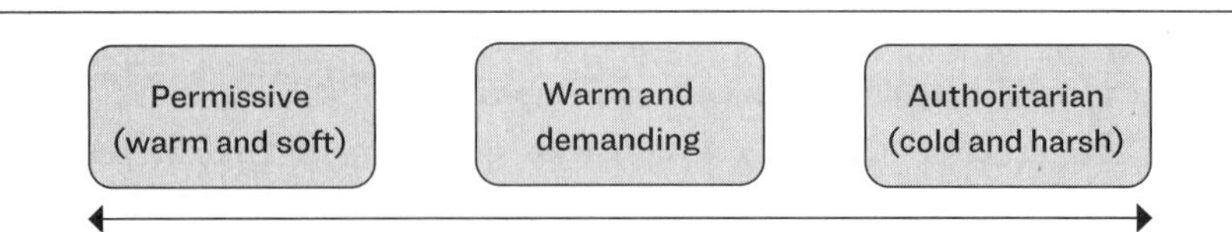

Strategies That Are Supportive and Empowering

We should also use strategies that are supportive and empowering. These relationships are characterized by teachers who are high in instrumental support and low in dependency.

- **Supportive.** There are many ways to give students the instrumental help they need to be successful. We can believe that all kids can grow and learn and hold them accountable for good work. We can value failure as an important part of the learning process and offer multiple pathways to success. When we differentiate academics and use diverse teaching methods, we ensure that all students have opportunities to learn.

- **Empowering.** We also want to help students grow in their abilities to be independent. We can make sure that students are engaging in appropriately challenging work, so they don't need excessive hand-holding to be successful. We can teach students strategies and skills to persevere and self-motivate. We can give students positive feedback that centers on how students did, not how we feel, helping them to feel stronger and more self-reliant.

Once again, these two characteristics are complementary. If we are overly supportive, swooping in and helping kids too quickly, we rob them of the chance to engage in productive struggle. Despite good intentions, we might lead kids into a state of learned helplessness where they are overly dependent on adult help. On the other hand, we know that the sink-or-swim method isn't supportive enough. To assign challenging work and then leave kids to figure it out on their own doesn't give the scaffolding students need to be successful (Figure 2.2).

FIGURE 2.2
Supportive and Empowering

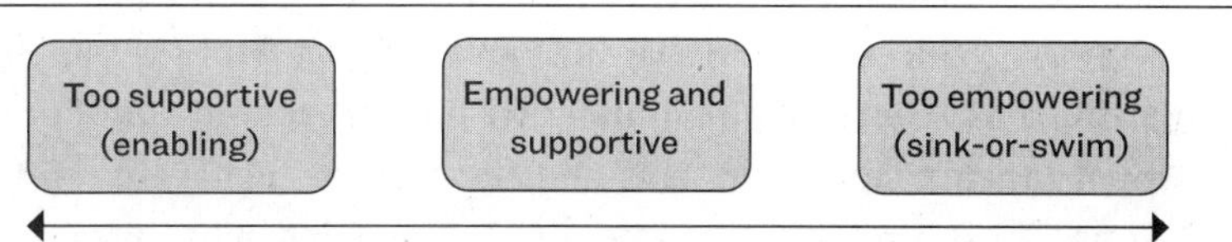

Using strategies that are both warm and demanding as well as supportive and empowering shows students that we care about them enough to hold them to high standards of learning and behavior. Students need to know that we're on their team and that, although we expect them to work hard and struggle, we're going to offer the good teaching and scaffolding they'll need to be successful. This is what all our students need, but it's especially important for our porcupines.

What If We Can't Manage a Positive Relationship? What's the Next Best Thing?

As much as we try to form a positive relationship with all students, it might not always be possible. After all, relationships involve two people, and students have important roles to play.

One group of researchers uncovered four different types of relationships formed between teachers and students and explored the impacts of each (Burns et al., 2022). Although this study was conducted with high school students in science classrooms, the findings mesh with my experience with children of a variety of ages (preK through graduate school) and in a variety of settings (swim teams, summer camps, classroom settings, and even parenting). Let's look at each of these four types in order from most to least effective (Burns et al., 2022).

1. *Positive TSRs* are warm and demanding, supportive and empowering. Teachers give students strong academic and socio-emotional support and avoid lots of conflict. These are the best types of relationships in terms of student outcomes.

2. *Complicated TSRs* are high in warmth and support but also high in conflict. Teachers may end up in a lot of power struggles with students, but they also form close connections with them. In terms of student outcomes, these are not as good as positive TSRs, but they're better than the other two.

3. *Distant TSRs* are low in conflict but also low in warmth and support. Although teachers don't engage in frequent battles with students, they also don't connect with them or give them much support. Students don't fare well in these types of relationships.

4. *Negative TSRs* are low in warmth and support while being high in conflict. Teachers do not connect with their students or offer them much academic support and end up in a lot of negative interactions. These are the worst types of relationships in terms of student outcomes.

It's not surprising that positive TSRs are best and negative ones are worst, but I think it's fascinating that it's better to have a complicated relationship with a student than a distant one. More positive school outcomes are associated with teachers who end up in a lot of conflict with students but who are also warm and supportive. It makes a lot of sense when I think about it. If we give up on a student ("Look, I won't hassle you, and you won't hassle me, and we'll just get through this semester"), they understand that we don't care about them. You've likely heard the adage "Kids don't care what you know until they know that you care." Teachers who connect with their students but also engage in conflict are at least showing they care.

Positive TSRs are the goal, but if you can't manage that, then it's better to be in a complicated relationship than a distant one.

There's another point worth exploring here. It might be easy to start thinking of *teachers* as positive, complicated, distant, or negative, but this isn't about teacher personality types. It's about *types of relationships*. These aren't the same. You could be a wonderfully positive person who ends up in a negative relationship with a child, or you could be a bit of a grump who creates a warm and supportive relationship with a student. You might have a complicated relationship with one kid and a distant one with another. Teachers who say, "I'm their teacher, not their friend," and "kids need to learn to work with different personality types" are onto something. We are not our students' friends, and there's plenty of room for a variety of teacher personality types. We can all practice the skills and strategies that are warm and demanding and supportive and empowering.

Common School Practices That Throw Gas on the Fire

In Part II, you'll read about practical strategies for building relationships slowly and steadily throughout the year. It's worth noting that there are a couple of common school practices that we should avoid. Although used with the best of intentions, they often disrupt the formation of positive teacher–student relationships.

Language of Conditional Approval

Many of us were taught to praise students in a very specific way: using the language of "I love the way you . . ." and "I like the way you . . ." when giving students positive feedback. The idea is that we can use our approval of children's behavior to positively influence their behavior. The better kids behave, the more of our approval they receive. This kind of praise shows *conditional* love for students. They get our approval and connection if they do what we want.

This can be especially problematic for porcupines, who often struggle to do what they should. The very kids who most need to know that their teachers care for them even when they're struggling get the least amount of positive emotional connection. They may notice that other kids are getting praised with teacher approval and reasonably conclude that their teacher likes the other kids more than them. This further pushes a wedge between us and our most challenging students.

In Part II, you'll hear some techniques to give students positive feedback in ways that show unconditional caring.

Room Removal and Who Helps Solve Problems

When kids are disruptive or are being unsafe, they may need to be removed from classrooms so they can calm down and regain their self-control. As the classroom teacher, you have a responsibility to teach the rest of the class, and you can't help a dysregulated kid in the heat of the moment. You need counselors and administrators to help out.

Where schools often struggle is in determining what the goal of room removal is and who helps kids process the problems that got them so dysregulated in the first place. Too often, room removal is viewed as a punishment. Whoever has the student when they're out of the room is expected to sort out what happened and help the kid get back on track. There are multiple problems with this system.

Punishments rarely help kids who are struggling—they just build resentment and further dysregulate already upset kids. The goal of removing a kid from the room should be to help them get their control back so they can reengage with learning.

It's also important to consider who should have a problem-solving conference with a kid who is struggling. In Part II, you'll learn a practical process for how to do this well. What's important to know for now is that a problem-solving conference is one of the greatest ways to build a positive relationship. When you take the time to sit with a kid, really listen to them, and help them come up with more productive and positive ways to handle what's getting in their way, they learn to trust you and see you as an adult to count on. Teachers must be careful not to outsource these conferences to administrators and counselors. Not only can you better help kids sort out what's going on, but you're the ones they need to have close relationships with.

A Look Ahead

In Part II, we'll consider tons of practical strategies for bringing this all to life, including the following:

- How to build relationships early, strengthen them throughout the year, and bring them to a positive conclusion in the spring.
- How to maintain, and even build, relationships through effective discipline.

- How to connect with porcupines' families.
- How to build porcupines' interpersonal skills.
- How to facilitate effective problem-solving conferences.
- How to support new students when they arrive mid-year.
- How to support students' transition to the next year.

Before we get there, we still have some important ideas to understand. Positive relationships are critical, but they're not separate from academics—far from it. After all, you come to school to help students learn and grow academically. It is also what porcupines desperately need. Many of them are struggling academically, and success with learning is their ticket to a productive and healthy life after school. So why do they so often resist learning?

Why Do Porcupines Resist Learning?

James faked asthma attacks when it was time to head out to the playground to write about nature as part of the science unit. Kelsey shut down during math, refusing to even try to solve word problems. Kevin won't even go look for books for independent reading time.

It's heartbreaking. Porcupines are often struggling with academics—it's one of the reasons they get so dysregulated. Why would kids spend more time and energy avoiding work than actually working? It seems to make no sense. It's like they're dying of thirst and refusing water when we offer it. They're going to exert effort one way or the other—why not try to get better at something instead of avoiding it? Why are our porcupines so often so highly skilled at self-sabotage?

The better we understand what drives this seemingly odd behavior, the better we can both empathize with and help our struggling students. That's the goal of this chapter.

Behavioral and Academic Struggles Often Go Hand-in-Hand

It's not exactly a revelation to say that kids who struggle with behavior also struggle with learning. But it is common to treat each of these struggles in isolation. Consider the following conversation I had with a school leader.

Dan, an elementary school principal, called me about working with his staff. "Mike," he began, "we're really struggling with management right now.

I'd like for you to come and work with my faculty about how to respond to student misbehaviors." I responded that I'd love to, but I had some questions. I wanted to better understand the situation. "Are all kids in the school struggling with behavior?" Dan responded, "Of course not . . . it's not all of them, but it's a significant number—maybe 20–25 percent." That is a lot. "Yikes," I responded. "I'd like to know more about that group. Are these also kids who are struggling academically?" Dan acknowledged that, yes, most of the kids who were struggling with behavior were also strug-gling academically. This wasn't a surprise. These two struggles often go hand-in-hand. "All right," I continued. "I'm wondering about the kids who are struggling academically. Are they getting to do really fun hands-on and project-based learning? Are they getting lots of choices about daily learning? Are they fully integrated into the regular work of the classroom? Or are they often pulled away from their peers to work with adults they don't know as well and given lots of rote skill-building work that has been broken down into such small bits that it's lost all meaning and interest?" Dan paused. "Um. I guess the second one." I responded: "I'd love to come and work with your faculty about how to respond to discipline issues, but we should also make part of that work about making the learning itself more engaging. If the work itself isn't worth doing, kids are always going to be melting down."

If we try to support kids who have challenging behaviors by just focusing on their behaviors, we may miss important reasons they're struggling in the first place. Let's not forget that most of the time kids spend in school is devoted to academic learning, so this is a huge part of the equation when it comes to supporting positive behavior and building positive relationships.

So *Why* Do Some Kids Resist Learning?

Relationships and behavior are connected with academic success, but this still doesn't help explain why some kids resist learning. In *Tackling the Motivation Crisis* (2021), I outline key psychological needs that all humans have, several of which have direct connections to this important question. Let's explore these briefly to better understand why some kids avoid learning.

Lack of Competence

I would love to be a great dancer. When I see dancing in a play or movie, I think, "I want to do that!" And yet I avoid dancing at all costs. Why? My (quite accurate, I'm afraid) perception of my dancing abilities is a barrier. I feel so incompetent that I don't want to work at getting better.

Sound familiar? Your students who struggle academically want to be good readers, writers, musicians, mathematicians, and so on. If you offered them a magic wand and they could simply tap their heads and be highly skilled, they'd do it. But their perception of their own incompetence is a barrier. They feel stupid when they struggle to read or to understand how fractions work. It's psychologically safer to not try than to try and fail.

Fear of Losing Belonging

The need for connection and affiliation is powerful, and it has been shown that students' sense of relatedness significantly affects their academic engagement and performance (Furrer & Skinner, 2003; King, 2015). Maslow (1943) placed this need second only to our most basic needs for food, water, shelter, and physical safety in his theory for understanding human motivation. If students worry that they'll be embarrassed in front of their peers, they may shut down, following the old adage that "it's better to shut one's mouth and risk looking the fool than to open it and remove all doubt." Again, it's often psychologically safer to not try. Similarly, if a student worries that to look like an eager student is a social risk, they might actively avoid schoolwork trying to maintain social status.

Lack of Autonomy

As we'll explore in more depth in the next chapter, porcupines are often highly sensitive to losing their power. Their lives are often out of control, so they're desperate for any control they can get. If they experience schoolwork as a series of exercises in compliance, refusing to do work may be a way to reclaim some of their power. In the novel *Holes*, Zero explains to Stanley why he won't talk to the counselors at Camp Green Lake: "I'm not stupid. . . . I know everybody thinks I am. I just don't like answering their questions" (Sachar, 1998, p. 99). When kids don't have any choice about what to learn, how to learn it, or how to demonstrate understanding of learning, it's almost impossible for them to be self-motivated. Too often in schools, kids get choices only after they finish regularly assigned tasks, or advanced groups or "gifted and talented" students are the ones who get the most project-based and choice-based learning. As in Dan's school, it's often the case that the more kids struggle, the more adults overstructure students' work, removing all power and control. It's no wonder some kids shut down.

Lack of Authentic Purpose

Many kids can be compliant with schoolwork even if they don't understand why they need to write up a lab report or learn the Pythagorean theorem. Porcupines often can't. They might moan, "Why do we have to do this?" or "When will I ever need to know this outside school?" School-work is so hard for them that they need a compelling and immediate reason to try—something more than "It's on the test," "It's for a grade," or "You'll need it next year."

Lack of Interest

All kids are curious about something. They have interests and passions—video games, sports, animals, and more. How often do they get to explore these curiosities in school? And how often do they have to learn about things they don't care about? I was observing a 3rd grade nonfiction reading lesson once, and a student (clearly a porcupine) dissolved into angry tears when he was handed his reading selection to practice: "I don't want to learn about *ants*!"

Lack of Fun

Our porcupines often struggle with doing things that aren't enjoyable. We all do, and a case can be made for the importance of learning to push through tasks that aren't fun. But how much of school should be like this? Students are more engaged when learning is fun, so we shouldn't be surprised when our porcupines quickly check out when it's not.

To be clear, many students may struggle with engagement when they lack autonomy, belonging, competence, purpose, curiosity, or fun, but they may be able to slog through it. They may have better skills of perseverance or a greater wellspring of energy from which to draw. They may be able to cope with small losses of autonomy, belonging, or competence because as a general rule, these needs are well met most of the time. They may be eating healthy foods and getting a good night's sleep. They might have the emotional reserves to handle work that's boring or too hard or too easy.

Porcupines, on the other hand, often don't have these skills or reserves. They often feel such deficits in these areas that they self-protect—they avoid engaging in work that seems pointless or makes them feel stupid, diminished in front of their peers, or submissive. So they shut down to avoid further pain.

Common School Practices That Throw Gas on the Fire

It's important to recognize that there are some common school practices that make these deficits in psychological needs even more acute. What's startling is that we often use these strategies intentionally with porcupines, not realizing that they're making things worse. To understand how these strategies feel from your porcupines' perspectives, let's consider how each might work if used in a professional development (PD) setting.

Imagine that you're a teacher who's struggling. Your school is engaging in a yearlong PD exploration in support of a new program. You want to do well, but it's been a tough year. You've had some personal challenges outside school that have made it hard to teach, and the new program isn't going well. You just can't seem to get to all the parts of the program at once. There's too much to cover. How would these strategies feel for you? Would they meet your needs for competence, belonging, autonomy, purpose, curiosity, and fun, or would they further erode them?

Ability Grouping

Teachers are grouped together according to skill level. "Low" or "weak" teachers are in one cohort. "Medium" or "average" teachers are in a second cohort. "Highly skilled" or "advanced" teachers are placed in a third. Of course, administration doesn't name these groups this way, but everyone quickly figures out what's going on. How would things go for the low group? Would teachers be highly energized and passionate about growth and learning, or would some feel ashamed and embarrassed? Would teachers in this cohort invest lots of time and effort into this new PD experience, or would they shut down and disengage? Would the group identity form around a sense of shared purpose about trying the new PD initiative, or might it actually form around *resisting* the new initiative? How would your professional morale feel if you were in this group?

Public Praise

You've been really trying to implement some of the new strategies you've been taught. You're gathering on an early release day for some follow-up PD. The district coach who had just observed your classroom saw you trying one of the new strategies, so she decides to give you a public shout-out. "I love the way Mrs. Sullivan has been trying one of the new peer-grouping strategies we've been talking about! Great job!" she gushes. How are you feeling right now?

On the one hand, it might be nice to be recognized, but you might also be a little embarrassed. If others in your cohort are not implementing the new program, you might worry you're being used to motivate them. Perhaps you worry about getting some dark looks or even ridicule from others in the group who are resisting the new approach.

Grading

Now let's imagine that the PD committee, in a well-intentioned effort to motivate and hold teachers accountable for implementation of the new curriculum, decides that they're going to grade teachers' work. Periodically, coaches, teacher leaders, or administrators will pop into your room to observe you in action. They'll have an implementation rubric in which they'll tally points according to how well you're doing. These points will be converted into a score that will go into your professional portfolio.

On one hand, you might feel more pressure to do what you're supposed to, but other thoughts might creep in:

- "Great, now, not only am I struggling to implement this new program, but I'm going to get a crummy grade on top of that! I'm already trying to do well . . . this will just make me feel worse!"
- "I guess I'll try to do what I'm supposed to when someone comes in to observe, but I'm just too overwhelmed to do it all of the time."
- "My permanent record? Whatever. I've seen plenty of teachers not implement new initiatives, and they're still here. What do low scores even mean?"

Homework

Acknowledging that there's a lot to learn in this new curriculum, the school's PD committee assigns homework to help people learn the new program. There are videos to watch, articles to read, and short reflections to write. None of these are overwhelming from the perspective of the PD team members, but you've already got some tough personal stuff going on at home. Just getting yourself to school each day is a struggle, and now you're supposed to do extra work outside school on top of everything else? Now, not only will you continue to struggle with the daily implementation of the new program, but you're probably going to fall further behind your colleagues as they deepen their learning through homework and you don't.

Scripted Curricula

There's one more element to this new PD approach your school is using that you find troublesome, especially as someone who is struggling. The people leading the program are following a manual as they help roll out the initiative in your building. They use the scope and sequence and read examples and FAQs provided by the program. Some of these examples are from different grade ranges and different settings than the one in which you teach, which makes the work hard to apply. Several times you ask why a certain strategy is better than the one you've been using, and you're told to "trust the program," which doesn't answer your question and deepens your sense that this curriculum doesn't have any personal relevance to you.

Of course, there are good intentions behind each of these common school strategies, but when viewed through the lens of the psychological needs of someone who's struggling, the potential downsides are clear. They might make people feel less competent, disrupt their sense of belonging, further diminish their sense of control, and not contribute much to an authentic sense of purpose. These are also just a few examples of common school strategies that may actually decrease rather than increase your porcupines' engagement and motivation. What others come to mind for you? Are there strategies and interventions commonly used at your school that seem to do more harm than good when it comes to your porcupines' learning and engagement?

It's Often Not About Will, It's About Skill

There's one more important idea to consider as you think about why your porcupines tend to shut down when it comes to learning. They often don't have the self-management skills, interpersonal skills, or academic mindsets they need to participate effectively in classroom tasks.

Your school or district likely has a framework that details the work-study practices it has identified as critical for student success. Many high schools and K–12 districts have developed "portrait of a learner" or "portrait of a graduate" profiles that detail the core skills and mindsets students should have to be successful. Many states have also adopted such frameworks. Several years ago, I analyzed dozens of different programs and approaches that were designed to support the skills and attitudes that students need to be successful in school. Figure 3.1 includes some of the self-management skills, interpersonal skills, and academic mindsets that emerged as I explored these various frameworks.

Are you teaching these skills to your students—especially your porcupines? And if these are the skills that students need to be successful with academic work, how are you embedding the teaching of these skills in academics? Too often, I see schools make one of two (sometimes both) missteps in this process. The first is that they devote incredible time and energy into coming up with their framework but little if any time in helping teachers learn how to implement it. The second is that they adopt some

FIGURE 3.1

Skills Needed for Success in School

Self-Management Skills	Interpersonal Skills	Academic Mindsets
• Metacognition • Reflection • Understanding one's emotions • Self-control • Managing impulsivity • Stress tolerance	• Social awareness • Perspective taking • Empathy • Collaboration • Cooperation • Conflict resolution • Collaborative problem solving	• Self-motivation • Growth mindset • Curiosity • Flexibility • Perseverance • Persistence • Integrity

kind of social skills program that's supposed to teach these skills outside of the academic curriculum. This doesn't work for a couple of obvious reasons. When an extra program is adopted outside of academics, it naturally competes with academics for time during the school day. Teachers are forced to fit it in, which often means having to decide whether to teach their already overloaded academic curriculum or the social skills one. Also, when these skills are taught during advisory or morning meetings, not during academics, they often lack academic context. You can't play a game designed to help build cooperation skills on Tuesday morning and expect kids to apply those skills Wednesday afternoon during a math activity. Instead, you should teach the cooperation skills Wednesday afternoon as part of the math lesson.

When your porcupines disengage or disrupt during academics, it might look like they don't care about learning, but it might instead be that they don't have the self-management skills of attention, frustration tolerance, and persistence required to engage in challenging academic work. Many students already come to school with a wide array of skills and strategies for working well with others, being flexible, managing impulsivity, and persevering through challenges, so they can handle less-than-great skill development in this area. Porcupines can't, so it looks like their fault when they cheat in games, melt down in frustration, or give up and shut down when challenged. After all, the other kids seem to do just fine—why can't they? It's a bit like not teaching explicit phonics instruction (which some kids can do without) and then blaming some kids when they struggle to learn to read.

A Look Ahead

In Part II, as you explore ideas for supporting your porcupines through-out the school year, you'll see many strategies to help support students' academic needs, including the following:

- Leveraging autonomy, competence, purpose, and belonging in daily work.
- Teaching the social skills, interpersonal skills, and academic mindsets your porcupines need to be more successful in school.
- Organizing your classroom space in ways that promote attention and regulation.
- Building academic stamina, curiosity, and excitement.
- Holding porcupines accountable for completing good work.
- Setting students up for success with new and complex academic structures.
- Grading to support high academic standards.
- Helping students handle school fatigue.
- Supporting students during spring testing.

Before we go there, there's one last big question we need to explore. Why do porcupines break rules? Why do they end up getting in so much trouble in school? This is important. In *The Explosive Child*, Ross Greene (1999) reminds us that our explanation guides our intervention, so we need to dig into the *why* behind kids' misbehavior. The better you understand what's really going on and get to the source of their challenges, the better you can respond in ways that are productive and supportive.

Why Do Porcupines Break Rules?

Kids are going to make behavior mistakes, and our porcupines will make more than their fair share. They're going to break rules. The way we respond plays a huge role in how porcupines feel about themselves, their schoolwork, and their relationships with us. Without examining this carefully, we might treat rule-breaking behaviors as something more than they really are. We might assume that kids break rules intentionally—when they don't. We might think that kids don't care about their schoolwork or classmates—when they do. We might slide into thinking of these behaviors as "bad" and might even start to unconsciously think of students who make lots of behavior mistakes as "bad." This will surely shape how we respond, which will play a large role in determining what kind of relationships we're forming with our porcupines.

Why Do You Speed?

"When you're driving, do you ever happen to glance down at the speedometer and realize you're going a little bit over the speed limit?"

This question is the kick-off to one of my favorite thought exercises I facilitate in workshops. When I ask this question to a room full of teachers, nearly everyone admits that they speed. I like to push this a little.

"How many of you keep speeding, once you realize you're driving too fast?" Most people raise their hands and chuckle. "How many of you speed almost every time you drive?" Again, most people raise their hands and laugh. "And how many of you plan to speed on your way home today?" Most people keep their hands up and laugh a little louder.

It's time to dig a little deeper, so I then ask teachers why they speed. I've facilitated this thought exercise dozens of times, and teachers answer in predictable ways:

- "Everyone else speeds—it would feel unsafe to actually drive the speed limit when everyone else is speeding."
- "Everyone knows you're not going to get a ticket if you're going 72 in a 65."
- "There's a good song on—I just need to go a little faster."
- "I'm preoccupied and thinking about something else."
- "The speed limit is too slow—it should be a 50 on that road—not a 35!"
- "I'm in a hurry, and I don't like to be late."
- "It's a habit. I don't even think about it."
- "I've got a new car, and it just floats along—I don't even realize how fast I'm going!"

As this list grows, teachers get more and more animated, laughing at the number of reasons they can come up with for speeding. It's also clear that this thought exercise doesn't elicit any guilt. If anything, people seem to feel more justified in their lawbreaking as the exercise proceeds.

I record their ideas on a chart as they share, but it's not until the end that I write the title at the top of the list: Reasons Students Break Rules (see Figure 4.1.)

FIGURE 4.1
Reasons Students Break Rules

- "Everyone else is doing it."
- "You can break the rule a little bit, and nothing happens."
- "In a good mood."
- "In a bad mood."
- "I was thinking about something else."
- "It's a dumb rule."
- "I didn't know about the rule."
- "It's fun."
- "Stuck in a habit."
- "I'm in a hurry."

Teachers gasp.

There are two key takeaways here. The first is to remember to have empathy for kids who break rules. Kids run in the halls, doodle on tables, don't pick up trash, sneak a peek at their phones under their desk, dawdle when settling into class, and engage in a variety of other rule-breaking behaviors for the same reasons we speed, have side conversations during staff meetings, and talk too loudly in the halls. Kids break rules for the same reasons that adults break rules. Let's remember not to be too high-and-mighty when considering what to do about it.

The second takeaway is to remember to not take things so personally when kids break rules. In all the years I've facilitated this thought exercise, not once has someone said that they speed because they're trying to annoy some deputy sheriff in the area. Yet somehow, when kids break rules, it's so easy for us to get upset—as if we have been personally wronged.

As it turns out, this isn't the only way that kid rule-breaking mirrors adult rule-breaking.

Psychological Needs

The same psychological needs that help explain why porcupines might resist learning can also help explain some rule-breaking behaviors.

Autonomy

Porcupines are often so sensitive to having their power taken away. Their lives may feel out of control, so they cling to any control they have and resist being compliant or obedient. Again, this isn't just true of porcupines. Lots of kids (and adults) don't like to be told what to do. Have you ever walked by a sign that says, "Do not walk on grass" and suddenly been tempted to walk on the grass? Teenagers are at developmental periods where they push back on authority as they strive for independence. When Procter & Gamble released public service announcements with famous people like Gronk telling kids not to eat Tide Pods, the number of incidents dramatically *increased*. ("Gronk's telling me to not eat Tide Pods? Well, now I kind of want to.")

Belonging

The need to fit in or to have connections with peers is a strong one. Kids may exert a lot of energy trying to gain approval from others or to maintain their social standing. Think of a time that you did something silly or stupid in the company of your peers. The need to be part of a group is strong, and it can lead anyone to do bad things. Again, this can happen at any age, but middle and high school teachers are probably painfully aware of how strong this impulse is during adolescence.

Competence

At a really basic level, this might explain why 5th graders jump to try to touch the frames of doorways as they walk through the hall. They're growing. They couldn't reach the doorframes last year, and now they can! Kids run where they shouldn't to see how fast they can go. Even something like swearing might seem like a "big kid" thing to do—a sign of maturity.

What happens when students feel a lack of competence—when they worry that they won't be successful? Might this, at least in part, explain why kids might cheat on tests or use AI to write an essay? Remember that some adults cheat as well. Think of performance-enhancing drugs in sports or companies that fudge quarterly earnings reports to show fake growth to shareholders.

The need for competence almost certainly leads some kids to apathy or work avoidance. If they worry that they won't be able to be successful with a school task, it's psychologically safer to not even try than to try and fail. They disrupt or shut down. Kids who need to practice reading avoid reading at all costs. Kids who need to practice working with others ask to work on the science task on their own.

Purpose

When kids don't see the purpose of work ("When are we ever going to need to know this outside school?"), they can be more apathetic. Again, as children get older and hit the tween and teen years, purpose becomes more important. Adolescents are less willing to invest energy in something just because they're supposed to.

Students might also be driven by a sense of purpose when breaking rules. They might say something mean to someone because that person hurt their feelings or was picking on one of their friends. They might lie about a mistake they made, trying to avoid a consequence. They might run in the hallway because they're late for class—just like you might speed because you're late for an appointment. They might be on their phones during class because they're checking in on a friend or sibling who is sick.

Curiosity

Curious natures and interests can sometimes be another reason someone breaks rules. Have you ever sneaked a peek at a sports score on your phone when you should be paying attention at a staff meeting? When you were a kid, did you ever get a magnifying glass and see what you could light on fire using the power of the sun?

Some students seem to need to explore "What will happen if . . ." when it comes to limits in the classroom. Educational psychologist Robert Mackenzie (2013) calls these students "aggressive researchers." We say that students need to clean up their area quickly so we can move on to the next activity, and they dawdle, needing to know what will happen if they don't do what we say. These students are probably operating out of a twin need for autonomy and curiosity.

Fun

Have you ever pulled out your phone to play a game during a dull professional development session? You know it's disrespectful of your colleague teaching the session and might distract others who are nearby, but you do it anyway.

It's fun to run in the hallway. It's fun to try to balance your cup of pretzels on your forehead. Playing Fortnite is more fun than working on a biology lab write-up.

More Basic Needs

The psychological needs for autonomy, belonging, competence, purpose, curiosity, and fun are important, but the base of Maslow's hierarchy includes a few other reasons why kids might struggle with behavior. When someone's most basic needs for food, water, sleep, clothing, and physical safety are not being met, their brain spends immense amounts of energy seeking to meet those needs, by any means necessary.

A kid who isn't getting enough food might steal other kids' snacks. A student who is deprived of sleep will be irritable and groggy. They may put their head down on their desk, not to intentionally disconnect from the social studies lesson or to be disrespectful, but because they are exhausted. There was a fight in their family half the night, or no one is making them turn their device off when they go to bed.

Impulsivity

When a student does something wrong, you ask them why they did it, and they respond, "I don't know," that response can feel like such a cop-out. Sure, sometimes "I don't know" is code for "I'm embarrassed to say" or "I'll get in more trouble if I say." But again, doesn't everyone do bad things every now and then—for reasons they can't quite explain?

Paul Bloom, a psychologist and professor at the University of Toronto, has taken a particular interest in why ordinary people who generally have a positive moral compass sometimes do bad things. I saw him speak once at the Learning & the Brain Conference in Boston, and he shared one way he's explored this topic: The Perversity Project.

Bloom put out a questionnaire online and asked people to share stories of times they had done something wrong simply because it was wrong. In his talk, he shared some of his favorite responses. One person shared of a time that he stuck his finger in a friend's ice cream before his friend could eat it. Someone else said that they like to walk on the grass where they're not supposed to. Another of his favorites was a woman who admitted to flirting with her friend's boyfriend, just to make things a bit uncomfortable.

You might hear these examples and wonder, *What is the matter with these people?* If you are typically compliant and rarely mischievous, these examples might make you question others' morality, but it's important to recognize that sometimes normally well-behaved people do things simply to be a little naughty. I'm reminded of a news story from several years ago, when the British Natural Environment Research Council let citizens have a hand in choosing the name of their new multimillion dollar polar research vessel. The runaway favorite name was *Boaty McBoatface*, a name that went viral after it was suggested by a BBC Radio personality. It wasn't the only goofy name suggested. Others included *It's Bloody Cold Here, Usain Boat,* and (my personal favorite) *What Iceberg?* (BBC, 2016).

If, right after these incidents of perversity, you were to pull these people aside and say, "Why did you stick your finger in your buddy's ice cream?" or "Why did you vote for 'Boaty McBoatface?'", don't you think these adults would likely blush, shrug, avert their eyes, and offer some version of "I don't know"?

Porcupines Have Even More Challenges

We have explored why any child might struggle with rule-following behavior in school. They will sometimes struggle to sit still just as we do during faculty meetings. They'll do the least amount possible to move on to more interesting and meaningful tasks, just as we might when filling out mandated paperwork that we think no one will read anyway. They'll push limits to exercise their autonomy and do knuckleheaded things to impress their friends.

As we explored in Chapter 1, porcupines have all of that going on . . . and often a whole lot more. Kids who are living on the edge of fight, flight, or freeze often respond more impulsively and more extremely when they feel threatened. Students struggling with a mental health condition or who are neurodivergent often respond to negative emotions or situations in unpredictable ways that confuse us. Students who don't have the interpersonal or self-regulation skills to manage the daily workload and communication requirements of complex learning can melt down or flare up more easily.

Common School Practices That Throw Gas on the Fire

Let's explore common strategies that we use with the best of intentions but that often make things worse for our porcupines.

Rewards and Punishments

Perhaps the most commonly suggested solution for kids who struggle with behavior in school is some version of carrots and sticks—rewards and punishments. Behavior management programs often recommend using incentive or reward systems. Kids are offered tickets or school bucks or stickers on charts if they're compliant with adult demands. These prizes are withheld when kids don't comply. Systems that emphasize punishments are nearly as common. Detentions, being sent to the office, and suspensions are meted out to kids who disrupt, and physical punishment is more common than many of us would like to believe. Did you know that corporal punishment in schools is still legal in 17 states and actively used in 14? According to data from the NEA, during the 2017–2018 school year, roughly 69,000 children in the United States were subjected to corporal punishment ("paddling, spanking, or other forms of physical punishment") (Greene-Santos, 2024).

The carrot-and-stick approach sometimes delivers short-term wins for adults, as students comply to get a reward or avoid a punishment. With the promise of a reward or the threat of a punishment looming, kids can sometimes muster the extraordinary effort it takes to get through a class period without blurting or walk quietly in the hall on the way to lunch, but these effects usually fade quickly. Consider these systems through the lens of the reasons that porcupines struggle:

- **Students experiencing trauma.** A school leader I work with often reminds staff: *We can't punish the trauma out of kids.* Corporal punishment is especially devastating for children experiencing abuse. Incentives are used based on the belief that they will motivate kids to try, so here we also see why carrots aren't helpful for kids experiencing trauma. Motivation isn't what's getting in their way.

- **Neurodivergence.** Similarly, kids who have conditions such as autism, Tourette syndrome, or processing disorder aren't struggling due to a lack of will. Their brains are wired in ways that often aren't being served well by the school environment. Carrots and sticks don't provide better learning environments. They simply try to force square pegs into round holes. For kids who have oppositional defiant disorder (ODD), carrots and sticks are simply felt as another way that others are controlling them (which they are). When I had a student with ODD, incentives and punishments were the last thing he needed, as they just gave something else to push back on.
- **Mental health conditions.** Carrots and sticks turn up the emotional heat. They make kids more worried (about not getting an incentive or about receiving a punishment), so they increase anxiety. Ross Greene states this clearly in *The Explosive Child*, his iconic book about working with easily frustrated and chronically inflexible children. He says, "Some parents find that such [carrot-and-stick] programs actually *increase* the frequency and intensity of their child's explosions and cause their interactions with their child to *worsen*. Why? Because reward and punishment programs don't teach skills of flexibility and frustration tolerance. And because getting punished or not receiving an anticipated reward makes kids more frustrated, not less" (1999, p. 78).
- **Skills and strategies that don't match expectations.** If you can't speak Russian, and I offer you a million dollars to speak Russian, will this incentive help you be successful? Would the threat of a punishment do the trick? Of course not. Incentives and punishments don't teach skills, so if your students are lacking the skills they need to be successful, they won't help.

Consider how these systems betray our low expectations. We wouldn't incentivize students if we thought they already wanted to do well. Without meaning to, we may actually send the message to kids that we think they don't care. Some kids end up living down to these expectations.

These systems also often create competitive social dynamics in classrooms. When students are being given points for good behavior, it's hard for them not to feel as though they're competing against each other. Some systems even promote individual and group competition to motivate students. I used systems like this early in my career and watched my porcupines pay a steep price. They were the reason I was using those systems in the first place, but they struggled to meet expectations more than most, so they were often on the losing end of reward systems. Demoralized and defeated, they started to sabotage others' chances of getting rewards and didn't even bother trying to earn the incentives offered. Punishments have the same effect, as porcupines see themselves once again on the losing end of the equation—unable to avoid getting in trouble. When teachers punish the whole group for the misbehavior of a few (the whole team loses bathroom privileges or the whole class misses recess), once again, porcupines suffer the most.

Signals for Attention That Control Students

Another common school structure that can be especially galling for porcupines is the use of certain signals to get the attention of a group. Consider the commonly used signals for getting the attention of students in your school. You may notice a lot of signals that require students to be immediately compliant, especially if you're in an elementary or a middle school. An adult claps five times (to the beat of "shave and a haircut"), and all students are supposed to clap back twice. Or perhaps an adult rings a bell, and everyone is supposed to freeze and raise a hand. An adult says, "flat tire" and the students hiss. A teacher says, "macaroni" and students complete "and cheese." At first glance, these sound playful and fun. But imagine someone using these in a professional development setting (which I have seen, by the way). You're in a partner chat with a colleague and are discussing a topic with great energy. You're in the middle of a sentence and someone calls out, "peanut butter" and you're supposed to respond "jelly" without finishing your thought. Are you feeling respected or disrespected? Are you going to comply, or will you quietly finish what you were saying?

Teacher-Centric Language That Emphasizes Compliance and Obedience

Common language habits emphasize teacher power and control while also emphasizing student compliance. Without even realizing it, the way we give directions, transition students from one activity to another, and encourage hard work might be especially problematic for porcupines. Consider these common teacher-centric language examples from the perspective of a student who is hypersensitive to their power being taken away and therefore likely to engage in power struggles:

- "*I need* you to put your book away and line up to head to lunch."
- "Try sounding out this word *for me.*"

- "In this next part of the lab, here are the two things you're going to do *for me*."
- "*I'm going to* give you 10 more minutes, and then *I'm going to* tell you what *I want* you to do next."

In Part II, you'll see many examples of language that emphasizes students' power and control rather than teachers'. You'll also explore many more discipline and management strategies that will support students' development of more positive and productive skills of self-management and social interactions, including the following:

- How to cocreate rules and routines with students.
- How to use consequences to hold kids accountable without being punitive.
- When and how to have a student removed from a classroom and how to help them reenter positively.
- How to teach your discipline systems to your students and their families.
- How to reduce power struggles.
- How to support "aggressive researchers"—kids who often test limits.
- How to adjust expectations to support students' success.
- How to maintain consistency through the end of the school year.

In Part I, we have explored who porcupines are and why they so often struggle in school on multiple fronts. This is important because we must have empathy for our kids who struggle. But empathy doesn't help us know what to do. That's what we'll dig into in Part II. After a brief introduction with some foundational ideas, we'll walk through the entire school year together, considering many practical strategies for supporting porcupines all year long.

PART II

Hugging Porcupines
All Year Long

Hugging Porcupines All Year Long

Now that we better understand who porcupines are and why they so often struggle in school, it's time to get into specific practices and strategies to help them have better school experiences. Before we dig into these particulars, there are a few foundational themes that are important to keep in mind all year long.

There Aren't Good and Bad Kids. There Are Kids Who Do Good and Bad Things.

When my son was running on the cross-country team in high school, it wasn't uncommon for someone to say, "Oh, your son runs cross-country? That's great. Those are such *good* kids!" Of course, this is a well-intentioned comment, and it seems harmless enough, but what does it mean when you say someone is a "good" kid? Do you mean they're kind, cooperative, and well-behaved? Do you mean they're well-groomed and well taken care of—that they come from a "good" family? If cross-country runners are the good kids, who are the bad ones? There must be bad ones if some are designated as the good ones.

I learned a lot about my son's cross-country teammates during the two years he was on the team. There were some kids who were often cheering for everyone (not just the fastest runners) during meets. There were some kids who offered others (not just the most popular kids) rides to and from team events. There were some kids who were often friendly and polite. There were also some kids who snuck into the woods during practice to smoke pot. There were some kids who participated in team hazing traditions that were hurtful and dangerous. There were some kids who left others behind on long runs and seemed to turn a cold shoulder on slower runners. And sometimes it was the same kids who did all of these things, both good and bad.

Remember that to be human is to be capable of great kindness and great cruelty. Also remember that students are still children. Were you ever irresponsible in elementary school? Did you do anything unkind when you were in middle or high school? Were you as fully developed then as you are now? It's not uncommon when I'm working with teachers to hear someone say of a student, "Well, you know, some people are just argumentative and disruptive—that's just how they are." No doubt, there are some kids who have built defenses around themselves or who have gotten into unproductive and disruptive patterns of behavior. But be careful about the temptation to make broad character judgments about the children you're responsible for helping. If you slide into patterns of thinking that amount to "some kids are good and some kids are bad," where do you go from there? What possible productive work can come out of this line of thinking?

All kids (and adults) can be kind, cooperative, self-motivated, and productive. All kids (and adults) can be mean, combative, lazy, and unproductive. All kids (and adults) are also capable of growth and learning. Your porcupines may be struggling with relationship, self-management, and academic skills, but they can learn. Your job is to help create environments in which kids can thrive and teach them the skills and strategies they need to be successful.

A Great Learning Environment Is Like a Three-Legged Stool: The Importance of an Integrated Approach

One of the things I find most frustrating about the way we're handling education today is that we often treat every problem or topic in isolation. The science of reading is somehow rarely connected with the science of learning. The way to teach math is somehow not connected with how to teach science. Programs promising to teach social skills are rarely connected with academics. Morning and advisory meetings are often seen as separate from the rest of the day. Perhaps this is due to how different companies, each with their own product to sell (math workbooks, literacy anthologies, science kits, social skills scope and sequence) are designing their work for their own little niche. Or maybe it's easier for schools and districts to try to solve one problem at a time. A holistic view or solution can feel overwhelming because it requires too much change all at once. However, the more we create silos and treat each challenge or problem in isolation, the more fragmented school feels for kids.

What does an integrated approach look like? Years ago, I heard Ruth Charney, one of my most important professional mentors, talk about how a great learning environment is like a three-legged stool (Figure 5.1). This really stuck with me and has informed my teaching ever since. It is such a clear visual image for the importance of an integrated approach. Consider that when one leg of a three-legged stool is wobbly, the whole thing topples over.

The seat of the three-legged stool is a great learning environment—a classroom or school where incredible learning can happen. Each leg, working in concert with the others, is foundational to that great learning environment.

- **Positive relationships.** Students and teachers have positive relationships with one another. Students have positive relationships with other students. Students' fundamental needs for inclusion and belonging are met in a safe community.
- **Engaging academics.** The academic work is worth doing, from the perspective of the students. The work meets students' fundamental

FIGURE 5.1
Three-Legged Stool

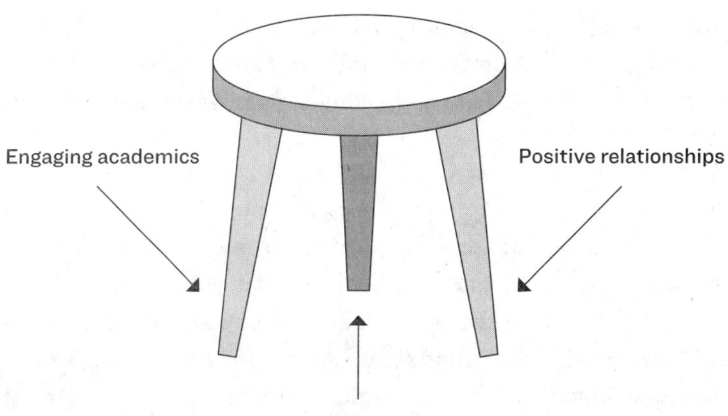

needs for engagement: autonomy, purpose, belonging, competence, curiosity, and fun.

- **Respectful discipline.** Students are taught the routines, procedures, and skills needed to manage themselves effectively. Teachers provide the structure and guidance needed for learning environments to be safe and respectful.

You might have positive relationships with your students and have respectful discipline practices, but if the academic work is boring, too hard, too easy, too sedentary, or unmeaningful, kids will disengage and (your porcupines in particular) may get disruptive. If the academics are engaging and you have positive relationships with students, but the discipline system is too permissive or authoritarian, you once again lose some of your students. If you have respectful discipline and engaging academics but don't have good relationships in the classroom, learning is limited. Kids will struggle to connect with learning when they don't connect with you or each other.

Focus on Teaching Self-Management Rather Than Managing Students

One of the biggest temptations to resist is to simply manage kids to get through the day. Although you'll always have to do some amount of managing, it's better to pour energy into designing systems and structures that enable kids to self-manage more effectively and then teaching them the skills they need to do so. It's a way you can follow the old adage, "Give someone a fish, and they'll eat for a day. Teach someone to fish, and they'll eat forever." Porcupines in particular will need a lot of structure and guidance to learn how to take academic risks, how to work cooperatively with peers, and how to recognize and manage their emotions. The more you can teach students the practical strategies and skills they need to engage effectively in school, the better you set them up for long-term independence and success.

Focus on What You *Can* Control

There's so much you can't control. You can't control whether your students have someone who reads to them at night or makes them turn off their phones to get to sleep at a healthy bedtime. You can't control what kinds of foods they eat or what kinds of influencers they follow online. You can't control whether their families set up spaces for them to do homework or teach them how to delay gratification or talk respectfully with others.

You can't control what their previous teachers or schools did with them or how much funding your school boards and town voters approve.

All these factors may affect your students' abilities to be successful in school, and you might, in the long run, work to support good school budgets, educate parents about healthy screen time and routines, or have conversations with other teachers and schools in the district about curricula to ensure that more students are able to read grade-level material by high school. Those are all worthy endeavors. But once your students walk through your classroom doors, all of that is beyond your control. You need to simply do the best you can with the kids you have.

What's Good for Some Is Good for All

My background is in classroom teaching. Although I now facilitate teacher professional development full time, I still feel and think like a classroom teacher. This book is written through that lens. Classroom teachers can't use strategies with some kids that are dramatically different from what they use with the rest of their students.

The ideas and strategies offered in this book benefit all students, not just porcupines. Many of the practices suggested in the following chapters clearly sit in Tier 1 of the multi-tiered system of supports (MTSS) framework. You might wonder about that given that this is a book specifically for kids who are more often associated with Tiers 2 and 3. In my experience working in schools for more than 30 years, first as a classroom teacher and now as a consultant who supports classroom teachers, I have found that one of the greatest challenges for porcupines is that we don't implement Tier 1 practices well enough. Although students who have less stress in their lives, more self-regulation skills, or stronger academic foundations might be able to tolerate wishy-washy language, looser discipline strategies, or more distant relationships with teachers, that doesn't mean any of these things are good for them. All children will benefit from warm and demanding teaching strategies. In *Troublemakers*, Carla Shalaby (2017) encourages us to think of students who struggle most as canaries in coal mines. They won't, or can't, endure school practices that feel unjust or dehumanizing. They alert you to changes you might make for all students.

Keep this in mind as you consider the ideas in this book. This book's strategies are helpful if you work one on one with a porcupine or if you're a classroom teacher who has 25 (or six classes of 25) students, some of whom are porcupines and some of whom aren't. All your kids will be better off if you use strategies that your porcupines in particular need to do better in school.

Hugging Porcupines All Year Long

It can sometimes be easy to think of relationship building as something to do early in the year. Once you've broken the ice and you know your students, you can spend the rest of the year digging into academic work. But it doesn't really work that way, especially with your porcupines. You may start to get to know your students even before they walk through the doors on the first day of school, but relationship building is a year-long endeavor. It's also deeply connected with the other two legs of the stool. Implementing a firm and fair discipline system and using engaging academic strategies require attention all year long, and all three of these legs look different at various times of the year.

The following chapters offer timely advice and practical strategies that align with various periods of the school year. I recommend flipping through this whole section of the book before the year begins. There are some pieces of advice, such as how to handle a new porcupine that arrives mid-year, that can happen anytime. Then, pick the book back up throughout the year to help guide your work with your porcupines.

A note about dates: In the United States, the school year begins and ends at various times, following regional practices. In the South and Midwest, school often begins in early August and ends in mid-May. In the Northeast and West Coast, the school year usually begins in late August or early September and ends in mid-June. You'll notice that in this month-by-month section, dates are offered in ranges to account for these regional differences.

Let's dive into the school year. In this next chapter, you'll explore some ideas to consider in late summer, before your students even arrive. That's when this important work begins.

6

The Last Weeks of Summer

July and August

The school year is about to start! Everything is fresh and bright, and it's exciting to know that you're about to meet your next batch of students. Amid this excitement, you might also have some trepidation. You know you'll have some students who are challenging this year. Perhaps you already know who they are. One year I knew a particular porcupine well before he arrived in my room. In that school at that time, we got our class list for the coming year at the end of the previous one. In May, I knew that Richard would be in my class next year, so I started to work on building a relationship with him right away. I had bus duty that year, so each afternoon, I made a point of chatting with Richard and trying to get to know him. "Are you playing any football this summer?" "Do you have any pets?" "Which friends will you hang out with once summer starts?" He answered my questions with as few words as possible and seemed eager to get on his bus. After several days of this, he stopped halfway up the bus steps, turned and looked over his shoulder at me, and asked (in a suspicious voice), "Why are you being so nice to me all of a sudden? Am I in your class next year or somethin'?"

Richard was definitely challenging at times, but overall, we had a great year together, in part because I took the time to really get to know him. Let's consider some practical strategies for how to set your porcupines up for a great year. This work begins in the weeks before the school year even starts.

Getting to Know Your Students

David Brooks, author of *How to Know a Person: The Art of Seeing Others Deeply and Being Deeply Seen*, argues that "there is one skill that lies at the heart of any healthy person, family, school, community organization, or society: the ability to know another person, to let them feel valued, heard, and understood" (2023, p. 9). This is perhaps your most important challenge early in the school year. We need to get to know our students. It's one of the essential ingredients in forming positive teacher–student relationships. Certainly, this is a primary focus of the first weeks of school, but you can begin this process even before the first day of school.

Create a Note-Taking System

It's easy to get overwhelmed with all of the information you need to learn about your incoming students. Consider creating a note-taking system. This will help you keep track of important information you learn about all your students, but it will be especially invaluable as you work to connect with your porcupines.

First, decide what kinds of information you want to collect. Make sure to focus on positive categories such as strengths, interests, friends and social connections, and family and background information. This kind of system can be especially helpful if you are a middle or high school teacher who works with more than 100 students each day or a special area teacher who might work with 500 or more different students each week.

Remind Yourself About Developmental Hallmarks

Have you ever received a new class in the fall and been surprised by how young your new students look? It's helpful to remember that even if you're teaching the same grade as last year, your new students are about 10 months younger than your previous students were in the spring. If you teach 6th grade, your last batch of students were 12 years old and moving into 7th grade. Your new students will be just barely 11 and are just moving up from 5th grade. That's a big difference.

Reminding yourself about child development can be especially helpful if you're changing grade levels. I remember the year I switched from teaching 5th grade to 3rd grade. My former students were moving into 6th, and my new ones were just in 2nd. They looked so little at the beginning of the year!

One of the reasons this can be so helpful is that sometimes common misbehaviors aren't really misbehaviors—they're just developmentally normal behaviors. Seven-year-olds are going to tell you when someone else swears. Fifth graders are going to jump to touch the tops of doorframes as they walk through the halls. Tenth graders can be upset one moment and silly the next.

There's a poster that hangs in an adult bathroom in a middle school in which I've worked (Figure 6.1). It's a reminder for teachers about what it's like to work with early adolescents.

FIGURE 6.1
What Is a Middle Schooler?

What is a middle schooler?
I was asked one day.
I knew what [s]he was,
But what should I say?

[S]he is noise and confusion.
[S]he is silence that is deep.
[S]he is sunshine and laughter,
Or a cloud that will weep.

[S]he is swift as an arrow.
[S]he is a waster of time.
[S]he wants to be rich,
But cannot save a dime.

[S]he is rude and is nasty.
[S]he is polite as can be.
[S]he wants parental guidance,
But fights to be free.

[S]he is aggressive and bossy.
[S]he is timid and shy.
[S]he knows all the answers,
But still will ask why.

[S]he is awkward and clumsy.
[S]he is graceful and proud.
[S]he is ever changing,
But do not be annoyed.

What is a middle schooler?
I was asked one day.
[S]he is the future unfolding.
So do not stand in the way!

Source: Anonymous.

To brush up on the developmental hallmarks of the age you teach, check out the CDC website: www.cdc.gov/child-development/resources/index.html. Although this information is geared toward parents, the hallmarks they offer are helpful for teachers as well. Another resource to check out is the book *Yardsticks* by Chip Wood (2017). It offers classroom and school specific information and advice for working with children ages 4–14.

Explore Student Files

I often didn't do this well enough when I was a classroom teacher. Some of my students had files that were so big that I got overwhelmed. Some had IEPs that were complex, and I would count on the first meeting with the special education team as my chance to get caught up on the basics. Don't do what I did—it wasn't enough!

Take time in the weeks before school starts to familiarize yourself with information passed to you from last year's classroom and special education teachers. There is important information in there about possible accommodations students might need, and if you're aware of these, you might be able to turn these accommodations into regular practices for all students. For example, if a student needs materials printed in a large font, you might always have a large-print option available with any handout that any student can use if they want. In this way you're supporting that student's need while making a more inclusive classroom that can better support other learners as well.

Talk with Last Year's Teachers

Perhaps one of the best ways to learn about your students is by talking with the teachers who had them last year. You might be leery of asking certain teachers about your incoming students, especially your porcupines. Some staff seem to relish venting about students they found frustrating, and you might not want to be negatively biased by their rantings. So don't ask those colleagues about those students. Or if you do, take what they share with a grain of salt.

Ask positive colleagues about challenging students' strengths and interests. Find out what strategies your colleagues found helpful with these students. Who did they work well with? Which peers do they struggle with? Is there anyone they should especially not sit with in the first few days of school? Is there another adult in the school—a counselor or art teacher or special educator—who they have an especially close relationship with? If so, make sure to interview that colleague next.

Bring your note-taking system with you as you talk with previous years' teachers so you can jot down all that you learn.

Connecting with Students and Families

You've probably heard that you never get a second chance to make a first impression. The way you introduce yourself to your students and their families can have, for better or worse, ripple effects that last all year. Once the school year gets going, you'll be quickly swamped, so consider reaching out to families late in the summer to introduce yourself and offer a chance to connect. As you do so, consider how you might be warm and demanding and supportive and empowering.

- **Warm.** Introduce yourself so that kids and families get to know you personally. Where did you grow up? What do you like to do outside school? What are some of your interests and passions?
- **Demanding.** What are some of the great learning units and projects you're tackling this year? What are some of the fun challenges kids will experience? What will students learn?
- **Supportive.** Share your teaching experience and qualifications. What are some ways you will help all kids learn this year?
- **Empowering.** How will kids grow over the course of the year? How will they become more independent? How will they be ready for the next year by the time they're done with this one?

Write an Introduction Letter

Consider crafting an email or a letter to mail to families introducing yourself. Use a light, friendly, and professional tone. Keep it relatively short and easy to read, recognizing that some family members might struggle with reading. Consider using Google Translate (or a colleague who can help) to translate the letter into the primary languages spoken by families, if you have that information.

Film a Video Introduction

Here's something you might do instead of or along with a letter of introduction. Record a video of yourself sharing that same information. Keep it short and the tone positive and light. Consider this as a chance for kids and families to see and hear how you're warm and demanding and supportive and empowering.

Hold an Informal Meet and Greet

You will likely spend a day near the beginning of the year working in your classroom. What if you invited students and families to pop by for a visit? You could designate just a few hours for this if you're worried about not being able to get much done during that time. I was always surprised at how many families would stop by to check out the classroom space and to meet me when I offered this. I often learned a lot about kids and their family dynamics during these times.

Recognizing That Classroom Design Influences Behavior and Learning

One of my favorite parts of being a classroom teacher was coming back to school in late summer to set up my classroom. Although it was a hassle to pack everything up so the room could be cleaned over the summer, I relished the task of setting everything back up again. It gave me a chance to reimagine the space. Where should I center the whole-class instructional space? Where will kids work in small groups? How can I create a space that feels cozy, so kids feel safe and comfortable? How can I create a variety of workspaces for kids who need to work alone or for ones who need to stand instead of sit?

There's a lot of research and literature available about effective classroom design, and quite a bit of it has to do with supporting learners who typically struggle in school—students with autism and ADHD in particular. Here are some ideas to consider.

- Large amounts of color can overstimulate and increase stress while monotone environments can create restlessness, irritation, concentration difficulties, and excessive emotional responses (Gaines and Curry, 2011).
- On-task behaviors can be lower in classrooms with more clutter and color variability (Godwin et al., 2022).
- A disorganized and cluttered space may be especially challenging for students with autism spectrum disorder (Hume, 2007).
- Cognitive engagement increases when classroom design matches instruction design (seats in rows for lecture, seats in groups for collaboration) (Sanders, 2013).

Effective classroom design is important for all students, but of course, it is even more important for our porcupines. Students who aren't easily overstimulated or distracted may be able to overcome a disorganized or chaotic space, but these conditions may make it almost impossible for some students to attend and stay regulated. One year, my students couldn't seem to transition smoothly. I'd have them put away their writing materials and get their math journals, and arguments and scuffles ensued. I eventually realized that the students weren't the problem. I had put all their cubbies where they stored their materials in one corner, and they couldn't physically fit together in the space. I moved half the cubbies across the room, and management problems virtually disappeared during transition times.

There's no one right way to design a classroom. A high school science lab, a middle school math classroom, and a self-contained kindergarten classroom will look quite different from each other. But there are a few design elements that you can keep in mind, regardless of the age of your students and the content you teach.

Flow, Space, and Accessibility

Is it easy to move around your classroom? Can students move from one area to another without bumping into each other? Will any of your students have specific space needs? For example, if you have an incoming student who is in a wheelchair, make sure to keep furniture spaced out so this student can maneuver easily. If you have students who aren't tall enough to reach certain shelves, keep everything students will need to access well within reach for all. If you have kids who are going through growth spurts, make sure these awkward and clumsy kids have extra space to maneuver around the room. One thing to keep an eye on is the amount of furniture you have. If your classroom space feels cramped, see if there are any extra tables or desks you could remove. Early in my career, I got rid of my big bulky teacher desk, and my whole classroom opened up.

Neat, Clean, and Organized

You may have been accumulating stuff for years, especially if you're a veteran teacher. A cluttered space makes it harder for everyone to learn, but some porcupines may be especially overwhelmed or overstimulated. Keep materials that aren't currently in action stored away in cabinets or other storage spaces. Keep your walls and even bulletin board spaces mostly empty, especially at the beginning of the year. You do not need to create elaborately decorated spaces for the start of the school year. (I'm especially talking to you, primary teachers!) Too many decorations, especially with bright colors, will almost certainly increase dysregulation in some of your students. Have materials clearly labeled. If different areas of the classroom have specific functions (such as a sink area in a science classroom or a library space in an elementary classroom), make sure the boundaries of that space are clear. You might place colored tape on the floor to designate a wash-up zone around a sink or an area rug in a library space. This can be especially beneficial for children with autism (Hume, 2007), but it's helpful for all students.

Color and Light

You may or may not be able to control the colors of your classroom walls. Some schools let teachers paint their rooms if they want to and others don't. Some allow teachers to bring in lighting from home while others worry about what the fire marshal might say. Do what you can. Even small design changes may have a positive impact on some of your most sensitive students.

- **Use muted colors.** Whether you're repainting your classroom or deciding on the background color for a bulletin board, use soft and muted colors. Avoid primary or overly vivid colors to promote more regulated behavior and better attention.
- **Use two or three colors.** Can you paint one wall a color that complements the other three? If not, perhaps you could use bulletin board backgrounds or other displays to offer some color variety. Avoid classrooms that are monotone or have too much color variety.
- **Use soft lighting.** Many teachers complain about the harsh white industrial fluorescent lights common in so many classrooms. Some people turn half the lights off to soften them. In a study in college classrooms, when fabric filters were placed over white fluorescent lights, it positively affected students' emotions, they reported fewer headaches, and they said it was easier to see the whiteboard at the front of the classroom (Yuen et al., 2023). This is such a simple and inexpensive modification to make to classrooms to help support emotional regulation and learning. You might even bring in a few floor or desk lamps to create a homier feel so you can turn off the overhead lights altogether at times.

Student-Centered and Learning-Centered Displays

Many of the ideas already shared in this section can help classrooms be warmer and more demanding, supportive, and empowering. For example, by labeling materials well and designing spaces with good flow and accessibility in mind, you can help empower students to be more independent in the classroom.

Another way you can support the kinds of relationships you're trying to build is by being thoughtful about what you display. How do you help students see themselves in their classroom? How do you help the room feel like ours (collectively), not yours (the teacher's)? How can you show that you value high-quality work? How can you emphasize positive classroom rules and expectations? How can you show that your classrooms are demanding spaces—where good work and behavior are valued?

To consider these ideas, think specifically about what you display in the classroom. You will make adjustments throughout the year, but you create your space before students even enter the room.

- **Rules and expectations.** As you'll see in the next chapter, creating rules *with* students (not *for* them) can help students be more invested in their classroom communities. But for the first week of school, I recommend having a placeholder on display when students first arrive—so they know that rules are valued and are on the way. This placeholder might be a display that says Classroom Rules but is blank. Or it might be a set of temporary rules that you have posted: Temporary Rules: 1. Be Safe. 2. Be Kind. 3. Work Hard.

- **Introduction displays.** Part of your work in the first weeks of school is to get to know your students and to help them get to know each other. There are a bunch of ideas in the next chapter. Some of these ideas involve having a display space in the classroom where students can share personal information or where you display some initial get-to-know-each-other work. Make the space for this kind of display before students arrive.

- **Display names.** Another way to help kids feel known and valued right from the start is to have their names displayed in various ways. If students start the year in assigned seats, have students' names already posted at their spots. In elementary grades, you might have names posted on coat hooks or cubbies where students will keep personal belongings. Simply seeing their names in the classroom helps students feel a sense of belonging in the space.

- **Eventual work.** Once students arrive and start engaging in academic work, you'll want some spaces to display that work. Displaying students' learning is one of the ways you show its worth. Have bulletin boards and display shelves empty but ready to go.

A Few Things Not to Display

If one of your goals is to keep classrooms neat, uncluttered, and inviting, it may also be helpful to consider what not to display. Here are a few ideas.

- **Decorations.** Don't try to fill every space with posters and displays simply for the sake of decoration. These can overstimulate and distract students.
- **Anchor charts.** Hold off on anchor charts (posters with reminders about key content or skills) at the beginning of the year. If the walls are covered with posters about animal kingdom terminology, how to solve order of operations problems, or different kinds of punctuation, they quickly become wallpaper that your students don't really look at. Post those charts when kids need them and they'll have more meaning for students.
- **Teacher-centric displays.** This is your classroom, so having a couple of family photos or having a poster of a favorite sports team near your teacher workspace helps you feel more at home. These can also be ways of connecting with some kids who might ask you questions about your kids or want to talk sports with you. However, resist the urge to decorate large spaces of the classroom with your own personal interest items. This sends the message that the classroom space is all about you instead of your students.
- **Snarky posters.** I'm sure people mean to be playful when they put up a "This Is a No Whining Zone" or "Best Months to Be a Teacher: July and August" poster, but consider the tone these set for students entering your classroom. They seem to say, "I expect you to be whiny" and "I don't like working with kids"—messages that are the opposite of warm and supportive.
- **Meet the one person responsible for your success.** This bulletin board idea went viral on social media a few years ago. Under the title is a mirror so the student can see the "one person" responsible for their success. Although there are good intentions behind this display, it's simply not true. Kids require guidance and support from teachers, friends, coaches, family members, and others for their success in school. For kids who are successful in school, this message probably feels pretty good. For kids who struggle in school, it may sound accusatory. They may read this as "meet the one person responsible for your failure."

Assigned or Designated Seating

On one hand, open choice seating offers autonomy and seems to offer belonging, because students can choose to sit with friends. That might be a good goal to work toward later in the year. At the beginning of the year, however, I strongly recommend assigned seating to promote safety and (paradoxically) belonging. Let me explain.

Have you ever felt the anxiety of wondering and worrying about where to sit in a group? Perhaps you've attended a professional development conference, and you have to find a seat as an audience member or at a crowded lunch area. Have you felt the relief of knowing there will be assigned seating at a wedding reception? (*Phew—I don't have to figure out who to sit with. I just have to find the card with my name on it!*) Having an assigned seat takes the pressure off of asking people you don't know well, "Do you mind if I join you?" Again, this is a great skill to have and one to build to as the year goes on, but this is a big ask on the first day of school. And of course, who are the kids most likely to struggle with finding a spot to sit? Our porcupines—kids who already often struggle socially. Kids with lots of friends and plenty of self-regulation and relationship skills will likely enjoy having free seating, but they'll also do just fine with assigned seats.

If you already know which kids may struggle in school this year, be especially thoughtful about their assigned seats. Have them in a spot where you can see them and help them easily. If you've collected information about who they get along with (and who they don't), try to set them up for success with positive and appropriate neighbors.

Protecting Students' Advisory and Morning Meeting Times

Even in schools where inclusion is the norm, some students may need to be pulled out of the classroom for certain supports and services. Special education teachers may want to pull small groups of students for specialized instruction. Counselors or school-based mental health therapists may need to meet with students individually once a week. In the days before school starts, some of these folks may arrive at your door to schedule these times. It's not uncommon for them to suggest pulling kids from morning meetings or advisory times.

There's probably never an ideal time for students to be pulled for special services. Even in schools that have designated blocks of time for students to receive extra support and help, kids with significant challenges need these times to make up learning from school absences, get more time to take summative assessments, or get extra one-on-one instruction for core academic work. And of course, no one wants kids to miss core instructional time for extra services. There's one time of day that I strongly recommend you consider as sacred, especially for your porcupines: morning meeting and advisory periods.

Porcupines often struggle with peer connections. They can sometimes feel like they don't really fit with the group, or they may need extra coaching and support around how to interact appropriately with their peers. This is why it's so important for them to be an integral part of the times that are designated for community building and social skill development. If a student who struggles is pulled from these times, think of the message it sends to both them and other students: They're not really a full-fledged member of the group. I would almost always prefer for a student to miss academic time than to miss advisory or morning meeting.

Creating a New Student Plan

You never know when a new student might appear at your door. And it's not uncommon for new students to be dysregulated. Kids moving to new schools are often going through major upheavals in their lives. Their parents might have split up or they might be moving in with extended family. A parent might have a new job that required relocation. Even for kids who are usually well regulated and have decent social skills, a mid-year move is stressful. In the January chapter, we'll explore a few ideas for how to support kids in these transitions.

One way to be prepared is to have a plan in place for what to do if (and when) a new student arrives. There are a couple of things you can do before the year even starts to get ready.

In self-contained elementary school classrooms, I've seen some teachers who keep a small box of materials set aside in a convenient spot. This box contains some of the essential curricular materials such as a math text, writing notebook, reading response journal, other academic texts, and perhaps a name tag. You might even consider keeping a class set of name tags handy so that you can all wear one for the first week that you have a new student—to help them learn everyone's names. A few other items might be a get-to-know-you survey, a welcome letter, a few stickers (just for fun!), and anything else to help your new student feel positive and welcomed.

In a middle or high school setting, where you have multiple classes of students a day, you might include the core text for the subject you teach, some basic writing supplies or math tools a student would need, a couple of pens or pencils, and an agenda/calendar or notebook. You could also include a friendly note where you tell them a bit about yourself and explain some of the key routines of the room.

These are, of course, just a few ideas. What else might you include? What other items might help a new student feel welcome?

You might also have an extra seat ready to go. If you have 24 students, have 25 seats set up right from the start. That way, if a new student shows up in a few weeks, you're not running around the school looking for an extra table or desk. This also helps the other students in the room be more ready to accept a new student when they arrive. Having an extra seat designated for a new student is a reminder to all students to be ready to welcome a new classmate any time during the year.

A Look Ahead: The First Weeks of School

Some of the strategies and suggestions about the first weeks of school are things you might want to have on your radar now. Which routines will you teach first? How will you roll out a collaborative rules process? Make sure to skim through the next chapter now to see if there's anything else you want to do before the kids walk through the door on the first day of school.

7

The First Weeks of School

August and September

It was the first day of school, and students were streaming into the room, some talking excitedly, some with eyes down just getting through the door. I recognized most of my students already. They had been just down the hall last year. I already knew many of their names. Then a student appeared who I didn't recognize. She was tall and heavy, and her face was set in a deep scowl. She was wearing a fancy dress, out of place among most of the kids wearing nice shorts and short-sleeved shirts. The dress was tattered at the bottom and dirty. Her mother and grandmother were next to her, also tall and heavyset, wearing similar scowls. They filled the doorway, making it hard for other kids to enter.

"This is Kelsey," her mother announced in a gravelly booming voice. She handed me a thick manilla envelope. "We just moved here. This is her file. She's got lots of problems." Kelsey's scowl deepened, and she glanced around her, clearly wondering if her new classmates were listening. I quickly took the file and smiled at Kelsey. "Welcome! Come on in. I'll help you get settled," I said.

Kelsey was one of the most challenging kids I had as a classroom teacher. She struggled academically and socially. She had an explosive temper that burst forth at the slightest provocation. As you can imagine, her home life was less than ideal. She had lived in a nearby town until two years ago, I later learned. Her mother told her they were going on a two-week trip to another state, and they came back two years later. Kelsey was often teased for her appearance and gruff nature. She had learned that the best defense was a good offense—so she was almost always on offense. On the rare occasion when she did let her guard down and would work pleasantly with a classmate, she was almost certain to sabotage the moment a few minutes later, slinging an insult and pushing the classmate away.

Let's remember how nerve-racking the beginning of the school year is for most kids. Even for students who are usually successful in school, it's normal to be worried. *Will my teacher be nice? Who will I eat lunch with? Will I have friends in my class? Who will I sit next to? Will I be able to do the work?*

For porcupines, the beginning of the year can be even more worrisome. They may come to school expecting the worst, especially if they are older and have had bad year after bad year. So how do you help kids like Kelsey in the first few days and weeks of school? Let's consider some ways you can start the yearlong process of gaining their trust, helping them feel safe, and building positive teacher–student relationships with them.

Going Slower Now to Go Faster Later On

One of the biggest mistakes to make early in the year is to try to rush things. It's tempting. You know how much you have to accomplish this year, and it feels like every moment counts, especially for kids who struggle in school. Go slowly now so you can go further faster later on.

Build Connection with Students

Do you remember the story of *The Little Prince*? It's one of my favorite books from my childhood. In one scene, the little prince wants to become friends with a fox, but the fox lets him know that it's not so easy. Foxes have to be careful around people. Trust and relationships take time. "'What do I have to do?' asked the little prince. 'You have to be very patient,' the fox answered. 'First you'll sit down a little ways away from me, over there, in the grass. I'll watch you out of the corner of my eye, and won't say anything. Language is the source of misunderstandings. But day by day, you'll be able to sit a little closer'" (de Saint-Exupery, 1943, p. 60).

Some porcupines, especially older ones, may be rightfully cautious about building relationships. They've been burned in the past. They have had bad experiences with teachers. They're hesitant to trust you or even get their hopes up for a better year. So don't push relationship building too hard— you might push them away as they self-protect.

Some students might need you to simply be nearby and show that you're safe, reliable, and kind. This can be hard, especially if you are a one-on-one support for this student. You might share a small bit about yourself without expecting any return sharing at first. Watch your student, and go at a pace they find safe and comfortable. You have all year to build a relationship with them.

Build Connections Between Students

In these first few weeks of school, start this process slowly. Have all students wear name tags so they can learn each other's names. When arranging seating, put porcupines next to kind and patient students, and avoid putting kids together who you know have had troubles in the past. During morning and advisory meetings, have students share simple information about themselves (favorite animals, sports teams, hobbies, etc.). Even sharing about these safest of topics may feel risky for some students. You have all year to foster deeper connections between students, so err on the side of safety in these first few weeks.

Give Students Time to Build Academic Stamina

Resist the urge to dive right into challenging work. This goes for all students, not just your porcupines. Kids need time at the beginning of the year to build school stamina. Don't forget how exhausting it is to navigate a school day at the beginning of the year. There are new adults and peers to meet, new routines to learn, and a new schedule to navigate. It takes a while to adjust to getting up early in the morning, and kids will be tired. Spend the first few weeks of school reviewing key content from last year, previewing new learning, exploring new materials, and setting a tone of academic curiosity and interest.

I remember observing a 1st grade classroom in January, and the kids were incredible. During a 40-minute literacy block, students read independently, wrote independently, read with partners, used the listening center, and met with the teacher for small-group instruction. Kids transitioned from one task to the next with minimal guidance and stayed engaged for the full period. I told the teacher how impressed I was with the students' self-direction. She laughed. "You should have seen them at the beginning of the year! We'd try to read quietly for one minute. I'd set a timer, and the kids would look at books. When the timer went off, they'd practically collapse with exhaustion. We'd play a quick game, and then we'd try for another minute. It took us a long time to get to this point!" It's easy to imagine what would have happened if she'd tried to get these kids to work for 10 minutes straight in September. They wouldn't have been able to do it, would have become dysregulated, would have started to dislike reading, and never would have come as far as they did.

Foster Academic Curiosity and Excitement

Many of your porcupines come to school worried about academic work. They've struggled in previous years. They worry they're behind where they "should be" and behind their classmates. They may be right. They feel incompetent, and it's almost impossible to feel motivated to work on something you think you're bad at. Consider your students who struggle with reading and how they seem to find creative and energetic ways to avoid reading—even though it's what they need to do to get better.

In the first days and weeks of school, in addition to moving slowly with content, spend time helping kids get excited about the work and learning that's on the way. Here are a few ideas to try.

- **Preview and explore learning materials.** I used to have students explore their math workbooks through a scavenger hunt. They had to tag sticky notes on a page with something they already knew how to do, something that looked complicated or challenging, and something they thought looked interesting or fun. You might also let students explore and play with some materials such as math tools (blocks, protractors, calculators, etc.) and art supplies (colored pencils, markers, etc.) before they use them for academic work. This also gives you a chance to help students know how to take care of materials so they'll last all year.
- **Take a class poll.** Share the major units or themes you'll be exploring this year (or semester or trimester). Have students take a poll where they indicate which ones they're especially looking forward to. Share the results with the class to help set a tone of eager anticipation for academic learning.
- **Collect questions.** This might be connected with the poll, but it doesn't have to be. Have students ask questions about topics and units they'll be exploring soon. What are they wondering? What do they hope to learn? Having students raise these questions before units start gives you a chance to think about how to address their questions in upcoming learning.

These are just a few ideas to get you going. I'm sure you can think of other ways to build academic interest and excitement. Consider how this helps set a tone of empowerment and demandingness ("You're going to do challenging and amazing work") while also being warm and supportive ("You're all getting to be successful in this first stage of our work together").

Encourage Student Interaction and Collaboration

Eventually, you'll want your students to engage in partner or small-group work. At the beginning of the year, keep this to a minimum, especially with students who come to school with social anxiety. You have plenty of time to get to collaborative learning, but if you go too quickly in the first few days, you might elicit some students' fight, flight, or freeze response, causing them to shut down or flare up. This will make it harder for them to collaborate later.

Keep social and academic sharing light and simple, especially in the first few days and especially in upper grade classrooms where students are often worried about being judged. (Grades 7–10 can be particularly rough!) For example, in a literacy block, you might want to have students start sharing about their favorite types of books. If it's going to be too risky for some students to share about favorite books out loud, you might have students raise their hands to share about favorite genres. ("Raise your hand if you enjoy action/adventure stories. Raise your hand if you like biographies. Raise your hand if you like historical fiction.") Or perhaps you want kids to start sharing questions they are curious about in your first science unit. Instead of having kids raise their hands to share ideas aloud, you could have everyone jot questions on note cards. They can pass the note cards to you, and you could read some of the questions out loud without attaching names to them.

Another way to start to build students' connections with each other is to create some display spaces in the room where students can share about themselves. You might dedicate a bulletin board to students' favorite books or genres to read. You might invite students to draw pictures of their families and post these on a board. You might create mini "fridge spaces" with electrical or painters' tape. Create a small box for each student around the room where they can display personal artifacts (pictures, drawings, etc.). Then have roam-and-explore sessions where kids look at each other's spaces to make connections.

Err on the side of caution when it comes to students working together early in the year, especially in the first few days. If you already know who your porcupines are, use them as a barometer. What level of interaction feels safe and appropriate for them? What can they handle? If you base levels of interactions on your most sensitive students, you're not hurting anyone else, and you're setting the stage for more interactive and dynamic collaboration later in the year.

Although you may be itching to go faster with some of these things, remember that you have all year to build connections and dig into important academic work. The year is a marathon, and no one wins a marathon by sprinting the first mile. Also consider all that you can learn about students through these early activities, including their academic strengths, interests, and needs. Check out their spelling and handwriting. Look at the kinds of questions they ask. Notice how they explore new materials. You can also watch students' interactions with each other. Who seems to be able to work with anyone, and who struggles? There's so much you can learn by simply observing students in the first weeks of school. Make sure to jot these observations down in your note-taking system, as suggested in the previous chapter.

Reaching Out to Families

The first weeks of school are a great time to reach out to the families of your students to make some positive contact. There's a good chance you'll be reaching out to your porcupines' families throughout the year. Invest time early in the year to build a positive base.

Make Positive Phone Calls

When Jaclyn Rohr (2022) was a first-year teacher, her principal encouraged her to make at least five phone calls a week to families in the first weeks of school. She was nervous but immediately saw the benefit. She remembers reaching out to the mom of a student who she knew had struggled with behavior the previous year. "Hi, Mrs. Michaels, this is Jaclyn, Jesse's teacher. I wanted to take a moment to let you know about something great Jesse did! Today during indoor recess, I noticed that he did such a great job including his classmates in the game he was playing and encouraging his peers to not give up even if they felt sad that they didn't win the last round." There was a stunned silence, and then Jesse's mom responded, a bit choked up: "Thank you! Hearing that my son made some great choices today is the best news this mom could have gotten today." Now an administrator, Jaclyn encourages her teachers to do the same. It's such a simple way to get the year off to a good start with families.

Write Positive Emails

Another way to reach out to families with positive news is to send a personalized email to each family. It doesn't need to be long. A few simple sentences, like the ones Jaclyn shared with Mrs. Michaels, are all it takes. If you know that families speak a language that you don't speak, you could use a translation program (such as Google Translate) to send the message in a language families can receive.

Send a Family Newsletter

Try sending a simple newsletter to families about once every two weeks. Keep these short, sweet, and specific (busy caregivers likely won't read long ones, and you don't have time to write them). You can use a simple structure all year long so that once you create your first one, you can cut, copy, and paste for subsequent ones. Keep a simple doc on your computer where you collect ideas for newsletters so you don't forget important items. In these first weeks, share some simple things that are going well and things you enjoy about this class. You have a great opportunity to set a positive tone for the year through these simple newsletters.

Try Other Ideas

Some teachers conduct home visits, where they schedule a time to swing by children's homes to meet families. Some schools hold a cookout to welcome families back in the first couple of weeks. There are tons of other ways to start building positive relationships with your students' families. A little bit of extra proactive work now may make challenges easier to navigate later in the year.

Setting Up Rules and Routines

A friend of mine likes to joke about her colleagues who get their class lists each year and say, "Oh! I hope I get a good class!" She smiles and quips, "You know, *hope* is not a classroom management strategy."

Many students may be able to get by without a lot of structure. They may be naturally compliant or merely need to hear a teacher say, "You need to be respectful when working with a partner." They may be able to read subtle cues about what is and isn't acceptable. In fact, when you were a student, that might be all that you needed to be successful with classroom expectations.

For porcupines, this isn't enough. They need to know why certain rules and procedures are in place. They're not able or willing to be blindly obedient. They might need to see and hear what it looks like to have a respectful partner chat or to hang coats and backpacks up neatly in the hallway. This kind of deliberate and explicit teaching of expectations and procedures is imperative for porcupines. They can't be successful without it. The good news is that all students benefit from this kind of proactive discipline.

The way in which you set up rules and procedures will of course depend on the age of the students you teach and the size and setup of your classroom. I'll offer a few ideas for variations of these processes, but I encourage you to think of the spirit of these guidelines and create a system that you think will best fit the needs of your students. If the term "rules" is one that you're uncomfortable using for some reason, you might use "norms" or "expectations" instead.

Create Collaborative Rules

Some kids feel about rules like Constance Contraire, the oppositional heroine of *The Mysterious Benedict Society*, does: "Rules and schools are tools for fools—I don't give two mules for rules!" (Stewart, 2007, p. 74). When rules are imposed by authority figures and they feel repressive, students might be justified in resenting them. Kids who are oppositional may try to push back on them simply because they challenge their autonomy.

Creating rules with your students is one of the ways you can establish a warm and demanding and supportive and empowering tone early in the year. The time spent creating the rules emphasizes their importance and gives you the chance to talk about rules over and over as you move through the process. I encourage you to start this process in the first few days of school but not to rush it. The time itself that's devoted to the process shows how important they are and emphasizes that you have high expectations for behavior. You're demanding. Creating the rules *with* students is warm, supportive, and empowering. You share power and control with students, giving them a chance to exercise autonomy, gain a greater sense of belonging to the group, and be successful with discipline.

Regardless of the ages of the students you teach or the size and structure of your class, there are a few steps you can follow to cocreate rules with your students. This is a process I shared in *Tackling the Motivation Crisis* (2021) as one of the key structures to help students internalize and be better able to follow class rules:

1. **Envision an ideal learning environment.** Have students generate ideas about what a great learning environment will look, sound, and feel like. Have students share some of their academic and social

goals for the year. This is a crucial step. It emphasizes the *why* behind rules. Rules aren't about doing what the teacher expects, they're about behaving in ways that will allow everyone to experience a great learning environment.

2. **Generate a list of possible rules.** Next, ask students, "What will we need to do to create that kind of amazing learning environment we just envisioned? How will we need to work together and treat each other?" Have students share a lot of ideas. I recommend stretching this step out over several different short sessions so students have time to think of lots of ideas.

3. **Consolidate the list of rules.** Students (and you for that matter) won't be able to remember a huge list of rules, so consolidate this long list into just a few. Keep them short and sweet and stated in the positive ("Be respectful" instead of "Don't be rude"). Again, consider stretching this step out over a few short sessions. In their book, *Rules in School*, Kathryn Brady, Mary Beth Forton, and Deborah Porter (2011, p. 38) share four common rules that often come out of this process: care for ourselves, care for others, care for our classroom, and care to do good work. If your rules have some variation on those four ideas, you have likely covered just about any behavior that may arise during the school year.

4. **Gain consensus.** Make sure students agree with the final version of the class rules. If some students have reservations, keep tweaking them so that everyone is on board. Post these rules so that they're easy for you and students to refer to. Make sure to emphasize to students that it would be unrealistic for everyone to follow the rules all the time. Everyone (teachers and students) will make mistakes. These rules are the guide for how to work together to create the kind of learning environment you want to build.

In my 15 years as a classroom teacher, I never used the exact same process twice. Now, as a staff developer working in lots of schools, I've seen and supported many teachers in K–12 settings with a variety of roles in this process. There are so many possibilities for how to make this process work for you and your students. Here are a few ideas to consider.

- **High school, special area, and special education teachers.** If you teach many different classes or small groups of students each week, you might use the four-step process with each group individually.

I've seen this work well for an art teacher I've worked with. She ends up with 25 different sets of rules that she hangs on a ring by the door. Each class that enters flips to their set of rules. Another approach is to have students in all classes generate ideas for a great learning environment and rules (steps 1–2). Then you consolidate all the ideas (step 3) into one set of rules for your room. Share the list with each class, and see if anyone has any tweaks they'd like to offer (step 4). Present the final list of rules in the following class.

- **Middle school or other team-based teachers.** If you and several colleagues share the same students throughout the week, it might make sense to have one set of rules as a team. You might each have one group of students go through steps 1–2 separately. Then, you might have several representatives from each class (or advisory group) consolidate all the ideas into a few rules for the group (step 3). That list can then be ratified (or amended if needed) by all groups (step 4).

- **Primary grade teachers.** Young children may not have many ideas in the first few days of school about what a great learning environment should be. They might also not yet have ideas about goals or hopes for the year. Consider having some placeholder rules for the start of the year and then begin this process a couple of weeks into the year.

- **For a group that's reluctant to share.** If you have students that will not participate in a class discussion early in the year, you can still use this process. Have students envision a great year and write down their goals (step 1). You can then create a master list (without students' names attached) to share with the group. Then, have students write down ideas for rules (step 2). Share this list with students and have them try to consolidate the ideas (step 3) into categories either on their own or with a partner. You can then consolidate all of these ideas (still step 3) and then share the final list (step 4) with the group for final approval.

- **For a group that has traveled together.** Perhaps you looped with your class. Or maybe you're in a small school with just one class of students per grade. You might still have students envision a great learning environment and share goals (step 1) based on the exciting year they're about to have. Then pull out last year's rules and have the class decide if they'll still work for the coming year (instead of steps 2–3). Have students offer suggestions for modifications and finalize any changes (step 4).

- **If you already have school rules.** If there are already good school rules in place, or if, for whatever reason, you don't want to have students cocreate rules with you, you can still build students' commitment to the rules. Have students envision a great year of learning (step 1). Then, bring out the school rules and have students talk about how those rules will help them create the kind of great learning environment they envisioned.

An important part of being warm as well as demanding when establishing rules is to keep talking about rules positively. This is especially important for porcupines who may be predisposed to think of rules as "things that get me in trouble." Consider the difference between "Let's think of some rules that will help us stay on track so we can work well together and all reach for our goals" and "What rules should we have so people aren't disrespectful?" Consider sharing the idea that rules are what allow games such as basketball and board games to be fun. When everyone knows the rules, games can be more fun for everyone. Early in the year, kids (and especially hypersensitive porcupines) are looking for clues about whether or not you like them and are nice. The tone you use during this rules process gives them important information.

Use the Language of the Rules

Here's another way you can help students who can be oppositional to not feel like they're giving up their power when they follow rules. Part of this is achieved through the creation process. If they've had a hand in creating the rules, the rules aren't about what the teacher wants, they're about the learning environment the class is working to build. This should be reflected in your language.

Think about the chart in Figure 7.1 from the perspective of a kid who is sensitive to maintaining power and control. How might it feel to hear the language on the left? How might it feel differently to hear the language on the right?

Not only is the language on the right less likely to elicit pushback from prickly students, it reinforces the importance of the rules that you all spent so much time creating.

Establish Routines

What are all the "little" things that kids need to know to navigate school during the first few days and weeks? These little things aren't little. If kids

FIGURE 7.1
Frame Expectations Through Rules

Instead of Framing Expectations About Teacher Demands...	Use the Language of the Class Rules
"In my class, I expect students to be on time every day."	"One way to show responsibility (rule #3!) is to be on time."
"I want to see children walking in a straight line and being quiet in the hall."	"When we walk quietly and orderly in the hall, we follow our rule about respecting other learners."
"I'm so disappointed in how you behaved yesterday when I was out for a meeting."	"You really had a hard time being respectful of our guest teacher."
"I expect you to put in your absolute best effort on this next research project."	"What's one way you can show great effort on this next research project?"
"I need you to treat each other with respect."	"Remember to work at treating others with respect."

don't know how to get your attention, how to travel from class to class, how and when to use the bathroom, or what to do for lunch, the first day or two can fall apart quickly. Invest time early on to help kids learn and practice the routines of school. This offers them the support they need so they can be more empowered and independent as the year goes on. Also remember that many of your "easy" students might be able to survive with minimal guidance. They'll figure out what they're supposed to do. Your porcupines need this explicit setup, and it's good for everyone else too.

Again, the way you set up routines will vary according to the ages you teach and structures of your learning environment. Here are a few general suggestions to help you get started.

- **Identify the essentials.** Think of day one. What routines do kids need right away? I almost always taught signals for attention first. If I couldn't get the attention of the class efficiently, nothing else was getting done. What else is a priority? Some of the other big ones include bathroom procedures, moving from one spot to another in the room, and passing out and putting away materials. You can't teach students all the routines of the room on the first day, so figure out the essentials and begin there.

- **Use the amount of scaffolding required by your neediest students.** Instead of thinking of your "average" student (whatever that means), think of your neediest students. What kind of instruction and support do they need to be initially successful with the routines you're teaching? Use that as a starting place for how you teach routines to the group. A little extra scaffolding for kids who don't need it won't do any harm. For simple routines, you might elicit ideas from your students (see Figure 7.2). For routines that need to be done just one way and that kids need to practice, use modeling (see Figure 7.3).
- **Cocreate some routines.** You can give your students more autonomy by having them help you create certain routines. For example, you might have younger students help decide where they should line up in the room before heading out as a group. Older kids could help you decide what the transition into class should look like. How much time should they have to relax or socialize before class begins? Would they like a thinking question or warm-up task to ease into academics?

FIGURE 7.2
Eliciting Ideas from Students

Teacher: I'm about to partner you up, and then you're going to have some short partner chats about the text. Let's review. What are some qualities of an effective partner chat?

Margo: You should look at each other.

Teacher: Yep. That's one idea. What's another?

Filipe: Share the air.

Teacher: Yes. Can you explain that?

Filipe: It means both people get to talk and share ideas.

Teacher: Mm-hmm.

John: You also shouldn't be mean to each other.

Teacher: Yeah. That wouldn't fit with our class rules, would it? So, how should we talk with each other?

John: Nice. And smile.

Teacher: These are some ideas that will help partner chats work well. Also remember to try to keep your conversation going for the whole time. You might ask each other follow-up questions or share new ideas. Let's get started!

FIGURE 7.3
Modeling

Step	Sample Language
Goal statement: Explicitly name what you are going to model and why it's important.	"I'm going to show you how to load a slide onto a microscope. Once you can do this safely, you'll be able to be more independent with our lab work."
Demonstration: Model how to load a slide onto a microscope. Don't narrate, just demonstrate. Move slowly and deliberately so students can see what you're doing.	"Watch me and see what you notice."
Reflection: Have students think about and reflect on what they saw. They might do this by talking with a partner, sharing ideas with the group, or even jotting notes. Affirm students' correct observations and redirect/ modify incorrect or incomplete ones.	Teacher: What did you see me do? Student: You moved slowly. Teacher: Mmhmm. Student: You used one hand. Teacher: I did. Which fingers did I use? Student: Your first finger and thumb. Teacher: Yep.
Practice: Give students a chance to practice what they have seen. Observe students carefully as they try the routine or procedure, and coach as needed.	"All right, now it's your turn. Try to remember all those things we've been talking about."

- **Practice, practice, practice.** It's not enough to set up routines. Kids will need lots of reminders and chances to practice. Devote a good bit of time to that early in the year to get into habits. Once these routines are established, they'll (mostly) run on autopilot.

Use Signals for Attention

One of the most important routines to establish in the first days of school is how to get the attention of the group. Many students are sensitive to being controlled. When they feel like someone is demanding their compliance, their inclination is to push back. Keep this in mind when choosing signals to use. You're going to use these signals a lot, so if you use ones that feel overly controlling, your porcupines may be triggered into defiance over and over again all day long. This might seem trivial, but think of this from the perspective of a student. You're working on a math problem or talking with a partner, and suddenly someone claps at you. In midsentence or in the middle of your math thinking, you're supposed to abruptly stop and listen to the teacher. Wouldn't this feel a bit disrespectful? All students will benefit from signals that are more respectful and realistic. See Figure 7.4 for some examples.

Teaching About Consequences

Imagine how frustrating it is for students to spend a lot of time helping to create the rules of the classroom only to have those rules (seemingly) ignored when they're broken. A crucial part of establishing a discipline system in the first weeks of school is letting kids know what will happen when rules aren't followed. I encourage you to do some proactive work here. Have a few class discussions or even structure a couple of activities to really dig into this.

Understand Natural and Logical Consequences

You can have high expectations and hold students accountable for good behavior without using punishments. Natural and logical consequences are an important part of how to do this (Anderson, 2018). Before

FIGURE 7.4
Use Respectful Signals

Signals That May Feel Overly Controlling	Signals That May Feel Less Controlling
Call-and-response signals • Teacher: One, two, three, eyes on me. Students: One, two, eyes on you. • Teacher: Peanut butter and . . . Students: Jelly! Signals where students are supposed to respond immediately • The teacher claps, and students clap back. • The teacher rings a bell, and students freeze. • The teacher raises a hand, and students race the clock to be quiet and have to raise their hand as well.	Signals that are gradual • The teacher raises a hand, and students come to a good stopping place in their work and then turn their attention to the teacher. • The teacher rings a chime, and students have until the chime stops ringing to bring their attention to the teacher. • The teacher quietly counts down from 10 or 5, and students are ready by the time the counting is finished.

we get into how to teach about these to students, let's review a few key ideas about each.

Natural consequences don't require any adult action or intervention; they simply happen if you let them. If a student doesn't wear a coat to recess on a chilly day, they'll be cold. If a student doesn't bring their instrument to school, they won't have it for band practice. If a kid cheats while playing a game, other students might not want to play with them anymore. Natural consequences can be great learning opportunities, as long as they're not overly damaging. You wouldn't, for example, let a 1st grader try to balance on the top of the play structure. A broken leg (or worse) is too harsh a teacher. Similarly, you wouldn't allow a high schooler to not do any work all semester without support or intervention.

Logical consequences, on the other hand, do require adult action. According to Jane Nelsen (2006), there are four criteria that must be met for a consequence to qualify as logical. The consequence must be related to the behavior, respectful of students, reasonable for the student to carry out, and revealed in advance, so students understand potential consequences before they're used. This is why I recommend teaching students about logical consequences proactively. Here are a few examples of logical consequences.

- Dominic damages the school bathroom. He comes after school to help repair the damage.
- Ava knocks another student's project on the floor. She must help fix the project.
- Suzanne chooses to use a wobble stool for independent reading, but she's spinning in circles and falling on the floor. She loses the stool and goes back to her regular seat.
- Michelle is playing a math game and getting too emotional—throwing cards on the table when she loses a play. She has to take a break from the game to cool off before rejoining and trying again.

In all these instances, teachers must use calm, clear, and respectful language when implementing the consequences. If a teacher were to lose their cool and slide into a negative judging tone ("Michelle?! What's the matter with you? You know you shouldn't get so wild when you're playing a game. Go sit at your seat!") a consequence that is logical now feels like a punishment due to the punitive tone.

There's an important difference between logical consequences and punishments. Punishments are designed to change behavior through a disincentive. Kids are supposed to think, *I'll do the right thing because I don't want to get in trouble.* Logical consequences are more like guardrails on a highway. They help stop problematic behaviors from escalating and help repair damage caused by mistakes. Punishments are intended to be the solution to a problem. Logical consequences are not supposed to, on their own, solve problematic behaviors. They allow you to keep safe and orderly classrooms and schools so you can use proactive teaching, problem-solving conferences, and other supportive strategies for longer-term solutions.

Use a Tone That Is Warm and Demanding and Supportive and Empowering

Perhaps the most important aspect of this process is the tone you set when discussing consequences. Even if you use natural and logical consequences, if you set them up with a "you don't want to get in trouble" kind of tone, they'll feel punitive. Instead, consider using a "we all make mistakes (myself included), and consequences are part of how we work to live up to the rules we created" vibe. I think it's helpful to acknowledge that you, the teacher, will sometimes stumble with the rules. There are days your temper may be short, and you may be less respectful than you should be. You might leave a messy pile of paperwork out on a table, breaking the class rule about keeping the classroom clean and organized.

Try having a class discussion or two about consequences where you invite students to think ahead about what might happen when rules are broken. Consider breaking this discussion into two parts.

What can be hard about following rules? Simply posing this question sets an important tone. It normalizes making mistakes. You're showing your students that you understand that most people can't be respectful, responsible, and organized all the time. Here are some questions you might ask to elicit rich discussion. There are no right and wrong answers. The goal of this discussion is to help set a tone of understanding about why rules are often not followed.

- "Which of the class rules that we have created will probably be easier for you to follow? Which may be harder, and why?"
- "When is it easier or harder for you to follow rules? For example, are there certain days of the week or times of day when it's easier or harder to be respectful and responsible?"
- "Where is it easier or harder to follow rules? Is it easier or harder in certain areas of the school? Is it easier or harder when special events such as field trips or assemblies are happening?"

What would be some natural and logical consequences that might happen when rules are broken? While the first part of the discussion sets a tone of warmth and empathy, this second part sets a tone of demandingness. Even though everyone makes mistakes, accountability is important. This is how you show that your rules mean something. Depending on the age and makeup of your class, you might have students generate a list of common examples of rule-breaking, or you might give them some examples. Have students share ideas for logical and natural consequences that might make sense.

Don't be surprised if kids are overly punitive as they suggest ideas. ("If someone draws on the table, they should stay in for recess with their head down!") Kids who are used to the carrot-and-stick approach will likely suggest punishments (detention, being sent to the principal's office, losing recess, etc.). This is a golden opportunity to help them understand how natural and logical consequences are different from punishments. I recommend focusing mostly on small and everyday kinds of behavior mistakes instead of big or dramatic ones. This helps students see that everyone will break rules and therefore everyone will experience consequences. This is important for your porcupines to understand. Here are a few examples.

- Someone doodles or scribbles on a table. (They have to clean it up.)
- Someone runs in the hall. (They have to go back and walk.)
- Someone leaves a mess on a table. (They pick it up.)
- A student says something mean to someone else. (They find a way to try to make the student feel better—perhaps through a kind action.)
- A student is spinning in circles in a chair with wheels. (They lose the chair and sit somewhere else.)

One of Jane Nelsen's criteria for logical consequences is that they're revealed in advance. Through the course of the year, you can't (and shouldn't) try to warn kids about possible consequences of their actions before you let them fall. ("Remember, if you don't play fairly in the game, you'll have to take a break from the game.") You'd be in a constant state of nagging and threatening, which would set a negative tone and make it sound like you were expecting kids to behave poorly all the time. When you help them understand the concept of natural and logical consequences early in the year, they're not surprised when they happen. They also have the emotional stability to rationalize consequences when they're not in the heat of the moment. They understand that they're fair, which sets them up to better handle them later on when experiencing them.

The fact that you're carving out time to help kids think ahead about consequences sends the message that this is important. It gives kids who need to know "what happens if . . . ?" some good initial information. Some will still need to test. That's fine. It's part of how they make sure you mean what you say and say what you mean. You will show that you're trustworthy by following through when they test.

Actively Coaching Students as They Settle into Routines

Imagine you're learning to knit. Your teacher has shown you a basic stitch, and you're practicing it as she sits nearby. What kind of feedback do you need? You probably want to know when you're on the right track and when you're not. Knowing when you're knitting a stitch correctly helps you repeat the move. Knowing when you're making a mistake helps you correct it before it becomes a new habit. Your students need guidance as they settle into the routines of the school year. The way you do this is important. Focus your language on what they're doing, not how you feel about what they're doing, to keep your relationship with them separate from their behavior. If your knitting teacher says, "I love how you're keeping your tension consistent!" you might worry that you'll disappoint your teacher if your stitches get too tight. Instead, she could say, "Your tension is really consistent. That will help projects keep a uniform shape." Nonjudgmental language is especially important for your porcupines.

Here are a few specific language tips to consider. See Figure 7.5 on page 82 for examples.

Notice and Name Successes

When students are doing well, notice and name it. Avoid generic praise such as "Good job!" Instead, use specific reinforcing language so students know exactly what was good about what they just did. This helps your language be supportive and empowering. Also avoid language that emphasizes your approval such as, "I love the way you just . . ." Judgmental praise can feel controlling to some students, especially ones who can be oppositional. It sends the message that relationships are transactional: Students get approval when they do what the teacher wants.

Instead, focus on *what they did* instead of *how you feel* about what they did. This empowers students as they see their accomplishments. You might also use the language of the rules as you reinforce students' actions. This sends the message that you're valuing the rules kids created, and positive behavior is about living up to those rules, not about complying with teachers' demands (which some porcupines will resent).

Avoid the Tallest Poppy Syndrome

There's an expression used in Australia and New Zealand for what happens when one person is put up above their peers. They call it the "tallest poppy syndrome," because the tallest poppy in the field is the first one to be cut down. So when we praise one student as an example for others to follow, we may inadvertently turn that student into a target.

This is a common management technique, but it's especially problematic for porcupines. This sounds like reinforcing language, but its true intent is to manipulate another child. For example, Jenny has come to her seat and has her book out, ready to go for her reading group. Matthew is nearby and hasn't settled or brought his book with him. Their teacher praises Jenny, "I like the way Jenny is sitting down and ready with her book!" She's not really talking to Jenny. She's talking to Matthew. This sets Jenny and Matthew up as competitors, and Matthew may become resentful.

Remind

You might use reminding language proactively or reactively. A proactive reminder is a friendly heads-up before students do something. You can also use reactive reminders. Kids are heading out the door, and you see some students start to rush. "Hey everyone, remember to walk slowly and keep your voices down in the hall." Students are working in a group and are forgetting to use the roles and protocols they've practiced. "It looks like your group is forgetting the protocols. Who has which roles in the group?" This is an example of an authentic question to ask. Be careful to avoid questions that aren't really questions such as, "Mike, is it a good idea to run in the hall?" This can feel condescending to some students.

Redirect

Sometimes your language should be clear, direct, and forceful. If something unsafe is about to happen, you should redirect. "Sarah, put the scissors down." Many students, especially ones who are used to directive language, benefit from directions that are clear and sound nonnegotiable. "Dustin, it's time to write. You can talk with friends later." When you use a firm and kind voice, you can be both warm and demanding.

FIGURE 7.5
Effective Praise

Instead of ...	Such as ...	Try ...
Generic praise	"Great job!"	"You were really focused during that reading period!"
Judgmental praise	"I love how you remembered to push in your chair!"	"You pushed in your chair—that keeps our room safe and neat."
Emphasizing compliance to teacher demands	"I appreciate that you just used kind language even though you're feeling frustrated."	"You just used kind language even though you're feeling frustrated. That fits with our rule about being respectful."
Manipulative praise	"I like the way Jenny is sitting down and ready with her book!" "Everyone look at how Mike is remembering to clean up his area before lining up!"	"Matthew, get your book and join us at the table." "Everyone, remember to clean up your area before lining up."
Asking a question that's not really a question	"What are you supposed to be doing right now?"	"Remember to get started on revising your writing."
Using wishy-washy language	"It's time to settle down for band rehearsal, all right?"	"It's time to settle down."
Asking a question	"Would you please put your snack away?"	"Put your snack away."

Responding to Initial Misbehaviors: Assume Best Intentions

These first few weeks of school are sometimes called the "honeymoon period" because kids tend to try hard to start the year off well. Even so, some of your porcupines might engage in behaviors that you need to address. As you are warm and demanding, let kids know that you assume best intentions. Here are a couple of examples.

I was asking students if they went by a nickname other than the name on the class roster. Charles went by Charlie. Elizabeth was Libby. I was writing down name tags for a class display and wanted to get kids' names correct. I got to Darren and said, "It's Darren, right?" He glanced at a friend with an impish twinkle in his eye and said, "People call me Bob." I was pretty sure this wasn't true, but I didn't want to call him out in front of the class and turn this into a big deal. I also didn't want to put "Bob" on his name tag. To do so could risk looking foolish in front of this new group. I winked at him and said, "I'll put 'Darren' for now and we can chat in a few minutes." Later that morning, I went over to Darren and said, "You were just goofing around with 'Bob,' weren't you?" He smiled sheepishly and said that he was. We both had a little chuckle and moved on.

Another instance felt more serious. In hindsight, the third week of school was too early to teach the class a morning meeting game that involved improv acting, especially because there were a couple of kids in that class that struggled with impulsive and inappropriate behavior. The game was called "What Are You Doing?" One person acts out a simple behavior (brushing their teeth, mowing the lawn, drawing a picture, etc.). The next person in line asks, "What are you doing?" The actor says something different than what they're doing. So if they're brushing their teeth, they might say, "Mowing the lawn." Whatever they say is what that next person acts out. It's a simple fun game designed to build community and practice creative and quick thinking. Later in the year, it can be used to reinforce academic content. I cautioned the group, "It's important to not ask anyone to act out anything embarrassing. It wouldn't be fine, for example, to say something like "Going to the bathroom." Allen immediately jumped up in front of the class. "You mean like this?" He squatted and made a giant pooping sound and laughed. The rest of the class looked surprised and some giggled.

What's the best way to go here? To reprimand Allen publicly and harshly is to invite a power struggle or more antics. Saying something like, "That's completely inappropriate! I can't believe you would do that in front of the class!" would have sent the message that I thought he was being disruptive on purpose, which might have damaged my initial relationship efforts. So I assumed that he didn't really think about what he was doing and was behaving with best intentions. "Allen, we shouldn't do that. Head back to your seat." I said this simply and firmly and then moved along with the game.

It can be hard to assume best intentions. Sometimes kids' outrageous behaviors seem so intentional and obnoxious. Here's why it makes sense to (at least pretend to) assume positive intentions. When I responded to Darren assuming he was just playing around, not trying to be disrespectful, I let him know that I was trusting him to be well-intentioned. It gave him an out, so he didn't need to flare up or shut down when I talked with him later. If I had accused him of being deliberately disruptive, I may have forced him into a corner where he either needed to submit or fight. If he really was being playful and I accused him of being deliberately disrespectful, I could have hurt his feelings by letting him know that I think badly of him. I'd rather be wrong assuming best intentions.

A Look Ahead: The Honeymoon's Over

In the next chapter, you'll explore some ideas for how to support students as they come off the high of the first few weeks of school. Many kids can use the nerves and excitement of the new school year to stay in control, but when this energy fades, they may have a harder time following rules and staying engaged. They may start to push limits, and negative behaviors might escalate. As academic work gets harder, students may become discouraged and shut down. You'll explore tons of ideas and strategies for heading off some of these things and helping kids stay more positively engaged in school, all while deepening your relationships with them.

The Honeymoon's Over

September and October

You'd think that after you get through the first intense weeks of school, everything would settle down and get easier. In some ways, it does. Students get more comfortable, and many routines become more automatic. You may notice that students' school stamina is building. They can sustain attention longer than they could a few weeks ago.

There are challenges that come with this time of year for your porcupines, however. Work starts to get harder and more complex, so students who struggle academically may start to feel more incompetent. Some students' nerves about school kept some of their impulsivity or prickliness in check for a couple of weeks, but as worries wear off, they have a harder time following rules. Paradoxically, as they start to feel safer, they may have a harder time self-regulating. If the first couple of weeks felt surprisingly easy with your porcupines, the honeymoon may be over. Let's think about how you can continue to be warm and demanding and supportive and empowering.

Supporting Aggressive Researchers

Chris had been pushing limits right from day one. He seemed to always be doing something he shouldn't. He dawdled when our class was trying to leave the room. He'd do little obnoxious things to distract other kids—flicking their ear with his finger, pushing their pencil away from them, and whispering at them when they were trying to work. He interrupted class discussions and lessons with irrelevant questions. We'd be in the middle of a math lesson, and he'd raise his hand as if to ask a question about content: "When's recess?" The schedule was posted in plain view.

Near the end of September, he did something that really had me scratching my head. His desk was near the front of the room about four feet away from our trash can. He had a small personal pencil sharpener filled with shavings, and instead of getting up and walking to the trash can, he dumped it all over the floor next to his desk. Argh.

Some kids need to know the answer to the question, "What happens if I . . . ?" They can't feel settled and safe if they don't know the boundaries, so they keep testing to see what the limits are. You may see some kids engaging in more of these kinds of behaviors once the honeymoon period of the first few weeks of school is under their belts. They're not trying to be "bad." They're trying to feel safe.

If kids are being aggressive researchers, give them the information they're seeking. Let them know that you do mean what you say. Show them what happens when lines are crossed. They're testing limits because they want to know what the limits are.

Reiterate Firmly and Clearly

Some students need to hear the directions again. They're checking to see if you're consistent. You say, "It's time to settle into your spot for advisory," and they don't settle in right away. Sometimes a simple and firm reminder or redirection is enough: "Tim, sit down for advisory." Be careful you don't slide into snark here ("Excuse me, Tim? Do you need a personal invitation?"). Even if this is meant to be gently teasing, you run the risk of sounding annoyed and sarcastic, which can damage the relationship you're trying to build.

Follow Through with Consequences

Let's return to Chris. I turned just in time to see him knocking the last of the pencil shavings onto the floor. I simply said, "Chris, that mess needs to be cleaned up before you leave today." The end of the day rolled around, Chris went home, and the pencil shavings were still on the floor. I talked with the custodian and asked him not to vacuum that area. The next morning, I called Chris's mother, told her what happened, and asked if she could bring him to school a few minutes early so he could take care of the mess. "When will you be there?" she asked. "I'm there now," I replied. Fifteen minutes later, Chris was walking through the door, his hair disheveled, holding a bagel with cream cheese. I said, "Go ahead and clean up the mess,

Chris." He did, and that was (mostly) the end of the limit testing for the year. He had the skills of self-control needed to be successful, and once he knew that I meant what I said, he could settle into 4th grade. He and I developed a great rapport that year.

It's important to follow through with consequences early in the school year. If you give kids lots of second (and third and so on) chances, you are teaching them that you won't follow through and that the rules don't mean anything. Remember, though, that consequences are only one part of a much bigger discipline picture. They help stop small things from becoming big things, and they can help repair damage done, but they can't teach skills.

Sidestep Power Struggles

The problem with power struggles is that there is a winner and a loser. If you win, the student may be resentful and start plotting how to retaliate, especially if this happened in front of peers. Both their needs for belonging and autonomy take a hit, and they may seek to regain these in unproductive ways. If you lose, however, you're potentially setting yourself up for more power struggles. Neither of these is productive in the long run. Although there may be exceptions, my rule of thumb is to avoid power struggles whenever possible (but when in one, win as gently as possible).

Here's a strategy that can help you either sidestep a power struggle or win gently, minimizing your students' sense of embarrassment and loss of power. I've found this strategy especially helpful with students who are strong-willed and defiant.

Sophie was at a table with a couple of friends. They were supposed to be writing. She was talking a lot and distracting others. I redirected once: "Sophie. It's time to stop talking and focus on writing." This helped for a few minutes, but it wasn't long before she was talking again. I walked over to her table and said, "Sophie. You're still talking. It's time to move. Get your writing stuff and head over to that table." I pointed to where she should move. Then, before she could argue, I moved to another group nearby and started helping a student with their writing. I positioned myself so that I wasn't facing Sophie, but I could still see her out of the corner of my eye. She huffed and rolled her eyes. She made eye contact with her friends at the table and rolled her eyes again. Then very slowly, she swept up her notebook, pen, and folder and got up. She huffed again and walked slowly over to her new spot, where she *very* slowly opened her writing and got to work.

I had learned that if I stood over Sophie and waited for her to comply with my direction, she'd simply fold her arms and stare me down. She would not lose a power struggle, especially with an audience of friends nearby. By giving a direction and then quickly disengaging, I was not giving her the chance to stare me down. By allowing her to roll her eyes and huff her breath, I let her keep a semblance of power in front of her friends, reducing her embarrassment.

Keep Your Cool

When Chris dumped his pencil shavings on the floor and didn't clean them up, I nearly blew a gasket. *What the heck was he thinking?* I screamed on the inside. When Sophie folded her arms and stared me down when I first tried to redirect her, I knew she was itching for a power struggle, and it was hard not to take the bait. I felt like my power was being taken away, and I wanted to fight fire with fire. But what does reacting with anger accomplish? Of course, you're going to get upset sometimes—you're only human after all. But whenever possible, take a step back, take a few breaths, and keep your cool. You're being a grown-up and modeling what it looks like to handle frustration in a calm and mature way. This is the very kind of modeling that many of your porcupines need.

Don't Give Away Your Power

What message do you send when you threaten to get another adult to follow through and enforce the rules? For example, if a teacher says to a student, "If you don't settle down, I'm going to send you to the principal's office," who is the teacher saying really has the power? The principal. If a playground monitor says to a student, "If you don't listen to what I'm saying, I'm going to tell your teacher," who really has the power? The teacher.

Instead, make sure to let the student know that you're the one who will follow through with consequences. If you do need to get help from another adult, make sure the student knows that you're the one initiating the consequence. For example, if you're a paraeducator supervising recess and a student is being unsafe on the playscape, you should let the student know that they need to move to a different area. If they say, "You're not my teacher! You can't tell me what to do!" you can reiterate that they need to move and say, "My job is to make sure kids are being safe. You're showing that you need to take a break from recess for a couple of days." Get help from a colleague if needed to remove the child from the playscape. (Losing recess privileges for a short time is a logical consequence for being unsafe at recess.) Then, before the child is allowed back at recess, they should meet with you to see if they're ready. In this way, they see you as the one who's in charge on the playground and will be more likely to respect your authority moving forward.

Removing a Student from a Classroom

At this point in the year, some of your porcupines may be doing more than simply pushing limits. They may be melting down. They may be flaring up. They may be getting aggressive. Of course, the goal is to help kids stay in your classroom as much as possible, but there are times when kids need more help than you can give them in the moment to calm down. You may need to have a student removed from the room.

When to Remove a Student from a Classroom

As a general rule, there are two times students should be moved out of a classroom: if they are becoming dangerous, either to themselves or to others, or if they are becoming so dysregulated that all teaching and learning in the classroom is being disrupted. Here are a couple of examples.

Mark was a 4th grader who could get volatile quickly. Several times already during the year, he had outbursts that hurt other children. Once when frustrated during a whole-class instrument lesson, he flung a recorder across the room, hitting another child hard enough to draw blood. Another time, when he thought someone had cut him in line, he impulsively kicked the other student in the stomach. One day, Mark was working with a group of students on a science research project. A group decision didn't go his way. When I looked over, he was sulking on the floor in the corner of the room. His neck and ears were flushed—a sign he was about to explode. He was stabbing a pair of sharp scissors into the carpet and dragging them back toward himself slowly. Stab, drag. Stab, drag. I walked over to him and positioned myself between him and his group. "Hey, Mark. What's up?" I ventured. He didn't (couldn't?) respond. He kept his head down and continued to stab and drag the scissors. This had the potential to be dangerous. I called for the two school counselors, and when they arrived, I had the rest of the class join me outside for a quick run around the playground. I wanted the counselors to try to get Mark out of the room without an audience, and if it got violent (which it did), I wanted to protect Mark from the humiliation of having his peers watch that. I also wanted to keep the rest of the class feeling safe. If they'd watched the full-blown meltdown, they probably would have lost the ability to learn for the rest of the day.

Alyssa was a 7th grader with a history of dysregulated behavior that could often be sexually explicit in nature. Teachers and administrators feared that she was being exposed to adult content (or worse) at home. She yelled in class, slung insults at other students from across the room, and defied teachers' directions loudly—eliciting shouts and laughs from classmates. During social studies class one day, she was particularly dysregulated. She had been fidgeting, twisting and turning in her seat, and making eye contact with others nearby, getting them off track. "Mr. Henry! Can I go to the bathroom?!" she bellowed as he was teaching. Mr. Henry patiently reminded her that she'd had a chance to go before class. "I didn't have to go then!" she protested. "Wait a few more minutes so you don't miss the lesson. Then go when we start the activity." She yelled, "But my panties are going to be all wet!" At this point, Mr. Henry had Alyssa removed so he could continue the lesson with the rest of the class. No one was able to learn social studies when Alyssa got this dysregulated. She was taken to the assistant principal's office with some work.

When Not to Remove a Student from the Classroom

Micah is a high school junior who often comes to class sleepy. He sits in the back of the classroom and puts his head on his desk when he feels overwhelmed. Sometimes he won't even respond to a teacher when they try to talk with him. This day, Micah is in a particularly grumpy mood. He stalks into class and immediately puts his hood over his head and his head on his desk. The teacher teaches the lesson, letting him be.

Jenny is having a tough afternoon. She came back from lunch in a sour mood. She was probably teased again. Her math teacher comes over to check on her when kids are working. "You seem upset this afternoon. Are you doing all right?" Jenny scowls and snarls, "This school f---ing sucks. I wish everyone would just die." She puts her head down on her desk. Her teacher reminds, "Jenny. Remember, language." Jenny keeps her head down. Her teacher backs off and makes a mental note to relay this information to the counselor who sees Jenny once a week.

In both instances, Micah and Jenny's teachers don't remove them from the classroom. Both students are dysregulated and disengaged, but neither is being unsafe, and teaching and learning can continue for the rest of the students. Although Jenny's comment about wishing people would die is troubling, there's clearly nothing to be gained by trying to talk about that now while Jenny's at code red. This is something to discuss with her later, when she's calm.

Strategies to Keep Students in the Room

Although some students may need to be removed from class, a few even on a regular basis, there are ways teachers can diffuse situations, helping students regain control before they escalate to unsafe or disruptive levels. If a student is starting to wind up (becoming defiant, disrespectful, disengaged, etc.), consider trying one or more of these strategies to avoid having them removed from the classroom:

- Take a break.
- Get a drink of water.
- Deliver a message to a colleague's classroom.
- Read a book.
- Color in a quiet spot.
- Take a walk.
- Take 10 deep breaths.
- Take a break in a buddy classroom.
- Have a snack.
- Listen to an audiobook.
- Use a yoga pose/stretch.

Suggested Logistics for Room Removal

If a student gets to the point where they are becoming unsafe or are so disruptive that teaching and learning is shutting down, it's time to act. This helps protect the child from themself and helps the rest of the class feel safe and move on with learning. The way in which you remove students has a huge impact on your relationship with them and with how the rest of the students react to the situation. This is a time when it's crucial to be warm and demanding. If you react in anger—"That's it, Zack. I can't take it anymore! Go to the counseling office!"—Zack can now be mad at you, and the rest of the class may now get scared and shut down. Additionally, if Zack is so dysregulated that he's being removed from the classroom, do you really want him heading there on his own? What if he punches a wall (or someone else)? What if he refuses to go and heads outside?

- **Exit procedure.** Ideally, the dysregulated student should be picked up or met by an adult who can make sure they safely get to where they need to be.
- **Location.** There should be a designated space (or two or three) in the school where kids can cool off. This might be a room, which can be especially helpful in a school where quite a few kids will need

this space on a regular basis. Or it might be a corner in the counseling office or a seat in an administrator's office. It should be private enough that the student doesn't feel embarrassed (e.g., it shouldn't be out in the open in the office) but also in a place where adults can keep an eye on the student to make sure they're safe.

- **Duration.** The time out of the room should be as brief as is possible—while still being long enough so that the student is ready to head back. This might be as short as 5–10 minutes. It could be much longer.

- **Break room strategies.** A variety of strategies might help students regain self-control while out of the classroom (see Figure 8.1). These will need to be tailored to the needs of individual children. They should be calming and soothing. Adults who are with them should be kind and polite but avoid strategies that might make a break feel fun or rewarding. This is not the time for a problem-solving conference, a strategy we'll get into in the next chapter.

- **Reentry.** Students should be accompanied back to class by an adult who can help with the transition back to the classroom. Students should be welcomed back by the classroom teacher with low-level positive energy (not with overexcitement and certainly not with negativity). Students should not be required to apologize or process what happened as they reenter. They should simply get back to work.

FIGURE 8.1

Strategies for Calming Down Outside the Classroom

Suggestions	Avoid
<ul><li>Word search</li><li>Sudoku puzzle</li><li>Crossword puzzle</li><li>Reading</li><li>Coloring</li><li>Computer time (soothing music, listening to a story, educational video, Inner Explorer, bio feedback, meditation, etc.)</li><li>Observe fish tank</li><li>Yoga poses</li></ul>	<ul><li>Candy</li><li>Competitive/exciting games (checkers, tic-tac-toe, etc.)</li><li>Getting stickers, toys, prizes</li><li>Computer time (energizing/exciting music, exciting video games, etc.)</li><li>Fun chatting/banter</li><li>Problem-solving conference</li></ul>

If you have a student who is struggling a lot, get help sooner rather than later. Check in with a counselor or administrator so they know what's happening. Ask teachers who had this student in previous years for suggestions. See if it's time to call for a team meeting to get others involved. There's still the misconception in some schools that "good" teachers can handle discipline challenges on their own. That's ridiculous. Everyone needs help sometimes, and "good" teachers know it.

Supporting Positive Academic Mindsets and Habits

If your porcupines struggle with academics (as many do), there's a good chance they have developed, or are developing, some negative mindsets about themselves as learners. This is natural. I have a negative mindset about myself as a dancer, even though I'm old enough to know that I could get better with deliberate attention and practice. Now that you're a few weeks into the school year, you are probably seeing evidence of these mindsets. Part of your relationship building can be about fostering positive and productive academic mindsets—ones that will empower students to be more confident, more open to feedback and learning, and more willing to tackle hard challenges without being overly reliant on you and other adults.

Notice Positives and Successes

Porcupines are often known for their struggles and deficiencies, and they often spend a lot of time in school focused on these. I can't imagine a surer way to discourage students or to discourage effort and motivation. It's hard to be motivated to work on something you think you're bad at, even if you know it's important.

So now that you're getting to know your students better, make sure to notice what they're doing well and let them know that you notice. If you want students to feel supported and empowered, use language that emphasizes their success, not how you feel about their success. Remember that teacher-centric praise ("I love how you're . . .") can go wrong in two ways for porcupines. For some, this feels manipulative (as it may actually be) and can lead to rebellion. For others, it may have the effect of students becoming dependent on this kind of praise for their sense of self-worth. They become overly needy.

It's also important that this feedback be authentic and meaningful. I was talking with a group of teachers about why "Good job!" wasn't specific enough to be considered effective feedback. A teacher, with a twinkle in his eye—he was making a playful point—said, "Yeah, but it's so easy to say, 'Good job,' because you don't really have to pay attention to what kids are doing." Yikes. So true.

Try noticing and naming what students are doing, without lots of judging:

- "You're really reading a ton today."
- "That lab write-up is neat and organized."
- "You're getting the hang of this. Those last three problems you worked on are all correct."
- "You're showing a lot of persistence on that piece of writing."

Don't be surprised if a student pushes back on your positive feedback. Some of them may be so used to failure that the idea of success is scary. Don't spend a lot of time and energy trying to convince them that they're wrong. Instead, simply share your observation and move on. For example, if you say, "You're showing a lot of persistence on that piece of writing," and your student retorts, "I'm not trying hard," you might shrug and say, "Oh, all right. It looked like you were working hard to me." Then, move on to another student or move on to the next topic.

Find Delight in Kids' Ideas

Jeffrey Benson is a lifelong educator who has spent his career supporting middle and high school kids who challenge us. He was first a classroom teacher and then an administrator, and now he serves as an education consultant. He is the author of several books, including *Hanging In: Strategies for Teaching the Students Who Challenge Us Most* (Benson, 2014), which I highly recommend. In an interview for an online course (Benson, 2021) I was building, we talked about how to help kids who have traditionally struggled in schools participate more in the classroom. He suggested several simple and powerful strategies: give wait time (15 seconds!) between when we ask a question and when we take a response, have multiple students share responses when we ask a question, and perhaps the most profound—find delight in kids' ideas.

Instead of always asking questions for which there are right (and wrong) answers—the "guess what the teacher's thinking game" as Jeffrey calls it—ask students, "What are you thinking?" He encourages us to be curious about what kids are really thinking about. What's in their heads? He says we need to be relentlessly fascinated by what kids are thinking. Imagine how it would feel to be a kid in a class, especially if you often struggle in school, to have a teacher who genuinely cares what you think. Imagine how warm, supportive, and empowering it would feel for a student to have their teacher show genuine interest in their thinking.

Share Why Kids Should Care

It's become common practice in many schools for teachers to post "I can . . ." statements in the front of the room. These statements alert students to the learning objectives of the lesson or activity—the *what*. Many porcupines (and plenty of other kids) also need to know the purpose behind the learning—the *why*. How does this lesson fit into the broader unit? Why is this information or this skill important?

Perhaps this is also a good time to remember basic good lesson design. The lesson begins with an initiation, something to hook learners' attention and build curiosity and purpose. Next comes the body of the lesson. This is the bulk of the lesson block and may include direct instruction, student practice, or assessment. Finally, the lesson concludes with a closing. This might be a quick recap, a chance for students to share takeaways, a look ahead to what's coming next, or any other mechanism for providing an emotional closure to the lesson.

If you don't build in an effective hook—if students don't know what they're doing and *why*—you shouldn't be surprised if they struggle to care about the learning of the lesson. There are so many other things to think about: tonight's ball game, the cute classmate sitting nearby, the video game to be played after school, or any of a myriad of other things. If kids understand the why behind their learning, they'll have a better shot of being more engaged and even being able to struggle and persevere when the learning gets tough.

Emphasize Student Ownership of Work

Kids who have experienced trauma or kids who are oppositional can be very sensitive to anything that seems to threaten their sense of control. In light of that, consider how these statements might feel to kids:

- "*I want you* to think about what you're going to write about in your journal."
- "*I'm going to give you* 10 minutes for this next discussion."
- "Here are the three things *you're going to do for me* in this next activity."
- "Try sounding out this word *for me*."
- "Here's what *I'm looking for* in high-quality work."

All these statements might be clear and direct, and they may be demanding, but they may feel *dis*empowering for students. In all these examples, the power and control clearly sits with the teacher, not the students. It's the teacher who owns the work, and the students' job is to do what the teacher wants. They either need to submit to your will—to be obedient—or they need to rebel—to refuse to do what you want to maintain their power.

A simple shift can completely change the way statements like this feel and may help students move forward with work: Put students, instead of yourself, in the center of the action (see Figure 8.2).

FIGURE 8.2
Who Owns the Learning?

Instead of Emphasizing Teacher Ownership . . .	Emphasize Student Ownership
"I want you to think about what you're going to write about in your journal."	"Think about what you're going to write about in your journal."
"I'm going to give you 10 minutes for this next discussion."	"You have 10 minutes for this next discussion."
"Try sounding out this word for me."	"Try sounding out this word."
"Here's what I'm looking for in high-quality work."	"Here are some things that will help your work be high quality."

Nip Negative Academic Habits in the Bud

This is also the time of year, as work gets harder, when students can start to get into negative or unproductive habits. They may start to disengage during class. They may drag their feet with in-class work and be less than productive. Some students might start to get behind on initial longer-term work such as writing projects. The longer you wait to address these kinds of initial struggles, the harder it will be to right the ship. These kinds of things have momentum, so try to nip them in the bud.

- **Reminders and redirections.** Jake is staring out the window and has lost focus in his reading. Give simple short verbal cues to help kids get back on track when they first start to struggle. "Hey, Jake. It's time to read." If you ignore these little things, they may turn into bigger things.

- **Check-ins.** Although it might be early for a full-fledged problem-solving conference, if you see a student start to get into a negative habit, have a quick chat to see if you can learn what's going on. "Hey, Jake. It seems like you've had a hard time focusing during reading the last couple of days. Is there anything going on that I can help with?"
- **Consequences.** Let small consequences fall early and quickly. "Hey, Jake. You're going to come in and do some extra reading with me tomorrow, so you can get caught up. Would you like to come in before school, during lunch, or during WIN time?" Letting consequences fall early in the year lets kids know that you're going to follow through on the class's rules and expectations.

Continuing to Build and Strengthen Connections

Building connections with students isn't something just for the first weeks of school. As the year progresses, it may be especially important to look for commonalities. One research study (Gelbach et al., 2016) found that when researchers showed teachers how they were similar to their students, those teachers perceived better relationships with their students, and those students' grades improved. The results suggested that this was especially true for underserved students.

Consider How Well You Know Your Students

After a few weeks of school, you are probably starting to get to know some students well, especially if you have been taking notes as you learn new things about them. Here's an activity to try to see how you're doing. I first learned about it in a workshop taught by Don Graves, one of the pioneers of the writing process (Anderson, 2016a):

Step 1: Name your students. Take a blank piece of paper or start a simple word document, and number the left-hand margin with the number of students you have in your class. (If you have 25 students, number the paper 1–25.) If you have more than one class, just choose one group of students for this activity. Then, write down your students in the order in which you think of them. Try not to go in alphabetical order or write down all of one gender and then another. Just this part of the activity can be interesting. Who comes to mind first, and why? Likely they are the ones who command your attention, either because of their strengths or challenges. Who do you struggle to remember? Why do you struggle to remember them? Are they quiet, compliant, or withdrawn? Once you have all students listed, move to the next step.

Step 2: What do you know about your students? Next, jot down something about each student that you know about them that doesn't have anything to do with schoolwork. *Tory likes horses. Macy's grandmother owns a quilting store. Rico lives with his dad. Andrew is into Minecraft. Kody loves to skateboard.* Are there students who you know well? Do you struggle to come up with anything for some? If so, you now know who you need to connect with a bit more.

Step 3: Do your students know that you know them? Now, make a check mark next to students' names if you have talked with them recently about that piece of personal knowledge. Why? Knowing your students is important, but just as important is making sure that your students *know that you know them.* After all, when students know that they are known by their teachers, they are more connected with school and will be more ready to learn.

Step 4: Fill in the gaps. Don't feel bad if you had some blank spaces on your paper. Even though I thought I knew my class really well, when I first tried this activity I was surprised at how much I struggled with a few students. Once you know that you haven't connected enough with several students, it's time to get to work. Find small moments to connect with them, like walking in the hall or when they first arrive in your classroom. Ask them about their Knicks hat. Ask what they did over the weekend. Tell them about your dog or something funny that happened with your nephew. Make sure to add whatever you learn through these small interactions to your ongoing list of what you're learning about your students.

Ask Good Questions

In *How to Know a Person*, David Brooks (2023) offers advice about the kinds of questions to ask someone to truly get to know them (pp. 92–93). In order to build trust and positive relationships, he suggests avoiding a few common types of questions. Questions that imply "I'm about to judge you" can be off-putting. Consider the judgment inherent in questions like "What kinds of grades do you get?" or "Are you good at baseball?" or even "What part of town do you live in?" He also advises against closed questions that allow for short answers. "Do you like math?" "Do you pitch?" "Do you live in an apartment?" can all be answered with a yes or no and likely won't elicit deeper sharing. Vague questions are also unhelpful. They may imply that you don't really care and aren't going to listen to a student's response. "How's it goin'?" and "What's up?" are the kinds of questions you might ask of a stranger as you pass by each other in a hall. They're not really meant to be answered except for perhaps a brief "Fine" or "Nothing."

Instead, Brooks suggests using humble open-ended questions. "Tell me how math feels for you as a student." "How did you feel when you made the baseball team?" "What's something you enjoy about where you live?" These kinds of questions show genuine social interest and caring. Students are more likely to feel like you really care when you ask these kinds of questions, and they're more likely to open up and share interesting responses.

Avoid Terms of Endearment

It's common practice in schools for some teachers to refer to students using terms of endearment such as honey, sweetie, pumpkin, dear, and kiddo. There are two reasons you might reconsider using these terms, and they both relate to relationship building, which is ironic, because you may use terms of endearment to show connection and affection with students.

One reason to avoid these terms is that they may inhibit your efforts to learn students' names. Especially if you work with lots of kids, perhaps as an administrator or special area teacher, you may use terms of endearment because you're not quite sure of a student's name. Knowing and using students' names is one of the most fundamental and important ways you show caring and connection. Make sure to put in the time and effort needed to learn all students' names and pronounce them correctly.

The second reason has to do with power. Autonomy is a prime driver for many of your porcupines. They often feel like they lack power and can get easily upset if they feel like their power is being taken away. Terms of endearment are almost always something that people with more power use with people who have less power. I was talking with a high school principal about this once, and she was curious. She often called students "pumpkin" and did so out of genuine affection, not as a power play. I asked her, "How would it feel if some of your students greeted you with "Good morning, Pumpkin!" when they entered the building in the morning. She had an immediate reaction, "Oh, that wouldn't work." Her eyes then widened as she realized, "Oh my gosh, I just imagined how it would feel if my superintendent called me 'Pumpkin.' That wouldn't be fine either!"

Even if you mean for terms of endearment to show affection and connection, they may not be received that way by your students. You can still show affection and connection by using a warm tone of voice and using students' names.

Building Students' Connections and Interpersonal Skills

In the first weeks of school, you helped students learn each other's names and build some initial connections with each other. Now, as the year is well underway, it's time to help deepen these connections and build students' skills and strategies for working with each other.

Increase (Slowly) Complexity and Depth of Morning Meetings and Advisory Activities

As students become more comfortable with each other and your community is starting to feel safer for all, you can start to introduce activities that feel a little riskier to morning and advisory meetings. These might include partner and small-group discussions or cooperative games. For example, especially by the end of this part of the year, kids might be ready for the activity Uncommon Commonalities. In this activity, students are placed in small groups (three or four is ideal). They are given a short amount of time (this varies depending on students' ages, but five minutes is a good ballpark) to see how many things they can find that they all have in common. Encourage your students to find specific or quirky commonalities. For example, a group might find out that they all have a sister, but if they dig deeper, they might find that they all have a younger sister with a first name that begins with a letter in the first half of the alphabet.

Avoid Competitive Games During Morning and Advisory Meetings

There is a time and place for competition in school. Later in the year, students might want to opt into a competitive game to practice naming the parts of a cell. Or you might play a whole-class Jeopardy-style game to review for an upcoming test. These can be fun ways for kids to practice content, and they provide a great opportunity for kids to learn how to win and lose gracefully. I strongly recommend, however, that you avoid competitive games during advisory and morning meetings, particularly early in the year and especially first thing in the morning.

Some kids get overly intense during competition and can have a hard time with emotional regulation. Kids who are already on the edge of fight, flight, or freeze (often porcupines) can lose control during competitive games or may have a hard time recovering from losing. These games also position kids as adversaries, which probably isn't what you're going for during these community-building times of day.

Use Your Most Sensitive Students as a Guide

When I was a newish teacher and trying to come up with lessons, activities, and games to use with my students, I often started with what I thought most kids would enjoy and be able to handle. This made a certain amount of sense. I was trying to engage the greatest number of students possible. I would announce that we were going to play Around the World, a competitive math fact game, and many kids would cheer (especially the ones who were already good at math facts). The problem with shooting for the middle is that the most sensitive students, the ones who struggle academically, socially, and emotionally, are often then asked to participate in things they can't handle. They get dysregulated, struggle (yet again), and fail (yet again), and other kids once again get frustrated with them, further decreasing their chances of being accepted and included later in the day.

Instead, as you're thinking about which activities to try, use your porcupines as your guide. Remember Kelsey, whose mother dropped her off on the first day of school announcing that she had lots of problems? I quickly learned that year that if the class was going to be able to enjoy any kind of group activity, it needed to be in Kelsey's wheelhouse. There were certain morning meeting and class meeting activities that I didn't do that year. Other times, I modified activities or gave Kelsey a different role. She was very sensitive to any physical contact, so I knew that The Human Knot, where students hold hands in a jumbled mass and try to untangle, wouldn't work. So Kelsey and I each served as coaches, walking between groups trying to untangle, offering advice.

When you use your porcupines as a guide for activities to facilitate with the whole group, not only can they be successful, but the whole class has a better experience.

Teach Students the Interpersonal Skills They Need to Be Successful

As you increase the complexity of activities with your students, make sure to teach them the skills they need to be successful. For example, if you want students to try sharing with a partner, think about the small strategies they may need to know to do this well. Do they know how to position themselves so that they can see each other? Do they know how to listen to a partner and really hear what they're saying? Do they know how to ask interesting follow-up questions or share thoughtful responses? Even something as seemingly simple as sharing with a partner has a remarkably complex set of skills involved. Although some students may know how to do these things (because they've been taught or they picked them up intuitively), many kids don't. I've watched even high school students struggle with this. We could blame COVID or technology or the ever-shifting landscape of family dynamics. Or we could not blame anyone or anything and just teach students the skills they need to be successful with the school activities we're having them do. Elicit ideas from students to have them share ideas to try. Model specific skills you want everyone to see and practice.

For more nuanced or complex strategies, try using the fishbowl strategy. Prep and practice the new strategy you want to teach the class with a few students ahead of time. Then, have them model the strategy with the rest of the class surrounding them (as if looking into a fishbowl). Pause the action every now and then to ask observers what they notice and what questions they have as their peers model the strategy. Then have the whole class try the new strategy.

Continue to Reinforce Successes

Make sure to notice what students are doing well and give them positive but nonjudgmental feedback to support their skill development. Remember to (usually) use second-person instead of first-person language to keep your feedback student-centered. Also, keep your feedback brief and don't overdo it. Some kids may feel manipulated if you're overly enthusiastic.

- "You two were looking right at each other as you shared. That must have helped you really listen well to each other."
- "That's it! You each were able to ask a follow-up question. Did you see how that helped extend your conversation?"
- To the whole class: "That was the best round of partner chats we've had yet. People were staying on topic, sharing interesting ideas, and responding with good comments."

Teach Productive Struggle

Christine Bergeron teaches at a K–8 school in rural New Hampshire. Many of her students come to her each year struggling with tumultuous home lives and past or ongoing trauma. She has seen how important it is to be warm and supportive so that her students know she cares about them and will help them. She also knows that for her students to be successful academically, they need to be empowered and to be held to high standards. One of the ways she does both is by teaching students about productive struggle.

This work begins in the beginning of the year. She has students engage in several collaborative challenges that are impossible. In one, students squeeze toothpaste out of a tube onto a tray and then work as a team to try to put it back in the tube using a toothpick. She lets students know that the task is really challenging, she intentionally uses nonacademic tasks (at first) to teach about productive struggles, and she keeps the time of the activity short. Students get about three to five minutes to try to get the toothpaste back in the tube. She wants the activity to be light and fun while still eliciting some frustration. She then leads a class discussion about how it felt to struggle so that students can voice how challenging it was.

Christine also shares some personal stories of her own about struggling with challenges. One of her favorites is a story about when she and her brother tried to dig a well when they were kids. She wants students to know that struggle is a normal part of growing and learning, and by sharing her own personal stories, kids get to know her (and trust her) a bit more.

She continues this work throughout the year, teaching students practical strategies for how to struggle productively (breathe, try again, ask for help, try a different way, break the task up, etc.) and eventually adding an anchor chart with reminders. She reads stories about productive struggle. She even teaches a nonfiction literacy unit in which students read stories about people who overcome challenges. When she starts to teach her students how to make effective learning choices, she'll use the language of productive struggle. "Think about today's math choice. Are you in a place today where you're ready for a productive struggle?"

When Christine was sharing about this work with me, she was adamant that, although she starts this work early in the year, building relationships with students and teaching them how to persevere through challenges is a yearlong process (personal communication, May 21, 2025).

Continuing to Practice and Reinforce Rules and Routines

The heavy lifting of the rule-creation process happens in the first few weeks, unless you work with very young children, in which case you're probably getting to that about now. But just because you've created rules with your students and taught many of the important school routines during the first few weeks, that doesn't mean this work is finished. Far from it! These next few weeks will in large part determine whether all the work you did around rules and routines was just a beginning-of-the-year exercise or the beginning of your yearlong work to teach discipline.

In these next few weeks of school—the time between the first weeks and the beginning of the holiday season—there's a lot of work to do to solidify what you've started.

Check on Class Rules

After rules have been up for a few weeks, consider checking in with your students about how they're going. You might create a class survey for students to fill out or hold a short class meeting. Ask students questions like, "How are our rules working for us so far?" "Are there ones that need any adjusting?" "Is anything missing—do we need to add any?"

This kind of check-in serves two purposes. The first is the obvious one. It gives everyone a chance to think about possible refinements to the rules. The other is that it once again brings everyone's conscious attention back to them, which reinforces how important they are.

Check on Routines

You might do something similar for routines. Invite students to give some feedback about which routines seem to be working well and which might need adjusting. You might also conduct a quick review yourself. As you think about the day, which routines are running smoothly and becoming automatic? Which ones are bumpy and need reinforcement or refinement? And how are you doing at being consistent with them? I often noticed that by mid-fall, I was starting to get lax with a few. I might have been good in the first few weeks about waiting until everyone was ready after I raised my hand for attention. As weeks went on, I would slip. I'd start to give directions when *most* kids were ready, which accidentally sent the message the students didn't actually have to stop doing what they were doing. I'd apologize to the class for letting my end of the signal slip and work at being better.

Teach New Routines

Think ahead about the next few weeks. Are there new learning structures you're about to introduce? Are there new procedures and routines that your students will need to learn? You might start teaching some of these now so that students are ready to use them well when it's time. You might even preview some of these with your porcupines. This can give them some extra processing and practice time so they can be successful when you introduce them to the whole class. For example, if you're going to teach a new sharing structure that students will use during writing, you might teach that new structure at the morning or advisory meeting as a social sharing structure. If you're going to use the fishbowl structure to teach that strategy, you could ask a student who sometimes struggles to be one of the students who models the new strategy. Teach it to them and coach them so they get extra practice and they're ready to model the strategy effectively for others in the fishbowl.

Holding an Open House

There's a good chance that you have an open house event during this stretch of the fall. This is such a wonderful opportunity to connect with families and make a positive impression. This is no small thing. Parents talk—at ball games, play rehearsals, in the grocery store, and in the neighborhood. And all this talk often shapes the reputation teachers have in a school, for better or worse. The more you can generate positive energy about your class and your teaching, the more likely it will be that parents share positive impressions of you with other parents, which makes them more likely to have a positive mindset about you. All of this can make you much more likely to have parents who are inclined to be on your side during the school year. Parents and caregivers of porcupines care deeply about their children, and they are often nervous about their children's teachers. Won't the year be better if these parents are excited that their child is working with you?

Send Invitations

It's not uncommon in schools for the parents who need to be there the most to be the ones who show up the least. As someone who sometimes hosts parent and family talks when I'm consulting in a school, I hear this frustration from many administrators and teachers. Why does this happen? Why are the parents who most need to be positively connected with school and who could most use the information about what's happening at school so often the ones who you can't get through the front doors?

There are likely a variety of reasons. Some parents may work evening shifts and can't take time off. Some may not be able to get childcare for younger children who can't be left home alone. It's also possible that some parents experienced their own school trauma as kids, and it's terrifying to walk through the front doors of a school. It's for this last group of parents in particular that you might consider sending invitations to the open house (though you'll, of course, send invitations to everyone).

Keep invitations concise and let families know what to expect at the open house. Give them a picture of what the open house will entail so they know what to expect.

Keep Talks Info-Lite

I remember once going to an open house when my daughter was in middle school. Her teachers put on a presentation that lasted more than 45 minutes. Each of the four teachers got up in front of the whole group and shared extensive slides about content students would be learning, school policy and procedures, and a myriad of other topics. They had a PowerPoint slide deck that must have had at least 30 slides, all packed with text. It was completely overwhelming. Don't do this.

Share a few important ideas in just a few key categories. You might consider using the three-legged stool as an organizing framework. Share a bit about how academics will be awesome, how you'll build positive relationships and a cohesive class community, and how discipline will be warm and demanding. If you have detailed information to share, create a handout or email so people can digest it at their own pace. What you say is important, but the tone you set is more so. Show that you're a good human and families will feel good about you working with their children.

Explain Your Warm and Demanding Discipline System

Parents and caregivers will be much more likely to be supportive of discipline (especially consequences) later in the year, if they have a chance to understand it before their kid is in the middle of a challenge. Parents can slide into fight, flight, or freeze just like their children. In my experience, explaining how your discipline system works early in the year helps parents be more open to and positive about your discipline efforts later in the year.

You'll likely have families with completely different beliefs and philosophies about discipline in your classroom. Some will want old-school harsh punishments while others may not want any kinds of consequences at all. Try to keep both extremes in mind when explaining your discipline system at the open house. For people who still have a "spare the rod and spoil the child" mentality, emphasize your demandingness: "I have really high expectations for good behavior. For us to have a great year together, kids need to know that rules matter and that something will happen when they're broken." And for the other extreme, lean into the warmness of the system: "I also believe that for me to have high expectations, I need to set kids up for success by teaching them how to work with each other and follow expectations. And when they make mistakes, the consequences will be logical." Be clear about the ultimate goal of discipline: "I want your children to be able to engage in great learning and to get the skills they need to be successful in school. We'll need a class of kids that can be respectful, responsible, and safe for that to happen."

I would then share a few simple examples of common behavior mistakes and logical consequences. I also let families know that I wouldn't be contacting them about all the little things that happened during the school day. However, I'd likely reach out to them if I needed help or advice, or if I was looking for family support for bigger or ongoing issues.

I'd always finish by letting them know that I was looking forward to our partnership this year, and I encouraged families to reach out to me as soon as they had questions or concerns. It was better to get ahead of little things before they became big things, I'd explain.

Share Successes and Joys About This Class

A great way to finish the presentation portion of an open house is to share some things you love about the group. Do they have a quirky sense of humor? Are they always asking tons of questions? Have they already done some cool work you're excited about? The more positives you share with families, the more positives they have to think about and share with others.

Give Time for Room Exploration and Informal Chit-Chat

If you have a one-hour open house, I recommend trying to keep your whole-group talk in the 10- to 20-minute range. That leaves a lot of time for families to explore the classroom. They can check out student work samples, see the organization of the classroom, and get a feel for the class. You might give families an optional scavenger hunt activity (that could be cocreated with your students) to help them notice the important things you want them to see. You can then mix and mingle with your students' families, answering individual questions and getting to know them a bit better. At the end of the evening, you might take a few minutes to jot down any newly learned student information in your note-taking system.

A Look Ahead: The Holidays Are Coming

By the end of October, kids should feel comfortable with the routines of school. They know what to do and are hopefully starting to let their guard down. They are likely feeling safer with you and with others. It's important to know that it's not uncommon for kids to struggle a bit more in the coming season. The holidays can be high stress times for kids (and adults) both in and out of school. In the next chapter, we'll explore how to handle the holidays with your porcupines.

9

The Holiday Season

November and December

Jayden was strong-willed with a streak of perfectionism that made him really frustrated when he wasn't good at something right away. In mid-November, he hit a wall in writing. We were trying our first attempt at fiction. It was a historical fiction writing unit that accompanied our study of the American Revolution, and given his love of facts, I had thought Jayden would love it. He was really struggling with the creativity aspect of the writing, however. He sat and stared at a blank page, his face and neck getting hot with anger. He crumpled his first draft and threw it on the floor. When I tried to confer with him, he put his head down, burying his face in his arms. His tolerance for frustration and his ability to push through challenges seemed to be dropping instead of building, even though the school year was well underway.

Shouldn't the school year get easier as it moves forward? And shouldn't November and December be a time of joy and anticipation? Shouldn't we all be in good moods as we look forward to the Macy's Day Parade, fall football, Thanksgiving get-togethers, and holidays such as Christmas, Hannukah, and Kwanzaa? If you've got a year or more of teaching under your belt, you know this isn't the case. The holiday season is right up there with the first and last weeks of school as one of the most stressful times of the year for students. Why?

There are several reasons this time of year is tough for kids in school. Although the holidays are a wonderful time for many, there's also a lot going on. Kids are taking trips to see family, or family may be coming to their homes for a visit. Even if these visits are joyful, they add stress to a household. And sometimes, the visits aren't joyful. Family visits may mean kids are sleeping on the couch and dealing with difficult relatives. Adults are scrambling—cleaning, shopping, juggling work and family responsibilities—and may have less time to spend with their children. They likely have shorter than normal fuses. Kids might have nervous and excited energy for the holidays, or they may be jealous and resentful, as they see other kids doing and getting cool things that they're not.

For kids who don't celebrate Christmas, this time of year can make them feel like they don't belong in schools that lean into Christmas celebrations. I talked with a mom whose son hates December in school. Their family is Jewish, and he's in a public school that still actively celebrates Christmas (decorating classroom doors, hanging lights in halls, putting up trees in classrooms, etc.). This mom is also a teacher in that same school district but feels like she can't voice her displeasure for fear of being "that person" who ruins fun for others.

This is also a time of high academic stress. For schools where the end of December marks the end of a semester, kids may be preparing for final exams or have big projects due. For everyone, the year is now really in full swing, and academic expectations are higher. Kids may be engaged in more group work and longer-term projects. Academic content may be getting more complex and abstract.

Of course, your porcupines may feel this holiday and academic stress more acutely than most other kids, and they may be less likely to reign in their excitement or deal with their anxiety. Let's consider some ways to help them during this tough time of year.

Adjusting Expectations

Let's once again return to Kelsey, who had that rough entry to my class on the first day of school. She entered the classroom most mornings with a thundercloud over her head, seemingly itching for a fight.

"Phoebe! You're wearing mismatched socks again! Why do you do that? It's so stooopid!"

"Mr. Anderson! You're talking about the Red Sox again? Baseball's stooopid!"

"What are you looking at, Hayden? Why don't you mind your own business!"

This was what a normal morning sounded like. Some days were worse—much worse.

As I worked with our school's counselor, Lisa, to figure out how we could help Kelsey be more successful in school—less combative, more relaxed, friendlier—we explored lots of ideas. A few seemed to especially help. They all involved adjusting expectations. Our goal was to give Kelsey as much time as possible in school with situations she could be successful with.

There were two times of day that were especially hard for Kelsey. The first was arrival time. I can't even imagine how uncomfortable and unpleasant the morning school bus ride was for her. She was often picked on by other kids, so she wrapped herself in a protective shell of anger, lashing out at anyone who ventured near. This was why she often entered the classroom in the morning spewing verbal assaults. It was about self-protection.

Fortunately, Lisa's office was only a few doors down the hall from where students who rode buses entered the building. The expectation for most kids in the morning was that they would enter the school and head right to their classrooms to be ready for morning meetings, which started just after morning announcements. I really wanted Kelsey to be able to join for morning meetings, because it was one of the ways I helped kids transition to school in the morning, connect with classmates in positive ways, and warm up to the academics of the day. When Kelsey came into the classroom flinging insults at everyone, she got other kids (and sometimes me) dysregulated, and it made it almost impossible for her to gain any of the benefits of morning meeting.

So we adjusted the morning arrival time expectations. Lisa's normal morning routine was to stand in her doorway and greet kids as they entered the school. She would keep her eye out for Kelsey and read her as she entered the building. What was her face and body saying about how her morning was going so far? If she looked particularly angry, Lisa would scoop her into the counseling office and help her get into a better emotional place before sending her to the classroom. She would then walk her to the room to make sure she came in appropriately. I knew that if Kelsey didn't arrive on time to hold off on marking her absent. She was probably with Lisa.

The other tough time of the day for Kelsey was the afternoon. Lunch and recess were hard to navigate. She struggled to find someone to sit with at lunch or to play with at recess. It was even harder for her to hold back mean comments or focus on challenging academic work (and nearly all academic work was challenging for her) in the afternoons. We typically ended our day with science or social studies work, and Kelsey didn't get a whole lot out of this time. She was surly and disengaged. Not only did she not learn a lot, but she made it hard for other kids to learn. We came up with another adjustment that helped a lot.

Lisa and I found a 1st grade classroom teacher who was willing to try an experiment. What if Kelsey could join her room a couple of afternoons a week as a special reading tutor for some 1st grade students who needed some extra reading time? How would Kelsey respond? Would she be kind and supportive or rude and combative? We weren't sure.

As it turned out, Kelsey was incredible. Perhaps it was because she was in a position of power, the older kid helping younger ones. Perhaps she wasn't worried about being negatively judged by 1st graders—who adored Kelsey simply because she was a "big kid." She was patient, kind, helpful, and nurturing. She came back to the classroom after these visits noticeably calmer and less edgy.

Know That Adjusting Expectations Isn't "Soft"

I struggled, at first, with how Kelsey was missing core academic content when she left the classroom, but as I reflected, I realized that she wasn't getting much of that content when she was in the room. Not only was she having a more positive experience as a 1st grade reading buddy, but she was also getting valuable practice reading, which was no small thing.

Some worry that adjusting expectations for students is being "soft" and that we should hold all kids to the same high standards. No doubt, all students need and deserve to be challenged and to have opportunities for great growth and learning. But all students are different, and if you have the same high standards for all kids, they'll be too easy for some and out of reach for others. It's important to balance being supportive and empowering. If work is too hard, kids often need too much spoon-feeding and hand-holding to complete work. Giving kids within-reach challenges and having realistic expectations is empowering because it gives them the chance to be more independent and successful.

Notice Patterns

One way to consider adjusting expectations is to look for patterns. At this point in the year, you're likely seeing your porcupines have successes and challenges at predictable times. Transitions are notoriously tough, whether it's the transition to school in the morning, lunch, recess, or the last few minutes of the day. These are all times when kids are moving from one place to another or interacting with different people in different ways. Or you might notice kids getting tired toward the end of a period or at the end of the day. Perhaps a particular subject, teacher, or area of the school is tough. Staying in control takes immense willpower, and after a while, students are too fatigued to hold it together.

These are just a few common patterns you might notice, but there are plenty of other possibilities. The key here is to notice these patterns so you can think about how to adjust expectations accordingly. Over the past few years, hundreds of teachers have taken online courses that I created about hugging porcupines, and many have shared examples of how they have adjusted expectations for their students. Figure 9.1 includes a few.

Take Stock of Homework

How much time and energy are you spending trying to get kids to bring in homework? This is often a huge struggle for porcupines, and you might consider adjusting this specific expectation.

First, it's important to know that short, simple homework involving skill practice does appear to have a positive impact on student learning at the high school level. Again, we can turn to *Visible Learning* and the work of John Hattie (2009). Overall, homework has an effect size of 0.29. (Remember that 0.40 is equivalent to a year's growth in a year's time.) In high school, the effect size is much stronger (0.64), and in elementary it's much lower (0.15). It might make sense to assign homework in high school and give students the support they need to be successful with it. For younger children, however, this isn't a practice worth the time, effort, and headaches it creates.

If possible, you might get rid of homework through middle school. If you can't do that, at least make sure that if your porcupines can't get their homework completed, it's not having a detrimental effect on their school experience. Some kids simply can't do homework, but they should still be able to be successful in school.

Holding Problem-Solving Conferences

When a student is having ongoing or repeated challenges, and reminders, redirections, and consequences aren't seeming to help, it's time to dig deeper. What's going on for this kid? Why are they struggling?

Problem-solving conferences are one of the most important strategies you will use to build relationships with students who struggle. They provide the perfect opportunity to be warm and demanding and supportive and empowering. September and even October may be too early in the year to

FIGURE 9.1
Adjusting Expectations

Challenging Pattern	Adjusted Expectation	Result
A student was frustrated with showing his work in math. He would rip papers and talk loudly and angrily about having to show his work.	He and his teacher met and agreed to solve a few (selected by the teacher) problems the "teacher's way" and others the "student's way."	The student became more independent, he finished more math, and there was less frustration for everyone.
A student was having a hard time getting to school for more than a day or two at a time and was falling behind in science class.	Each day she was in school, she and the teacher picked something to achieve, whether or not it was on that day's agenda.	The student felt more productive and knew she was on her way to achieving higher goals within the class.
A student with crippling anxiety sometimes missed weeks of school. They got so far behind in their resource room work that they felt overwhelmed.	The teacher allowed the student to choose what to work on when they returned to give them some autonomy and competence.	The student at least got some work completed and made some progress.
A student had a hard time sitting still in class.	Each day, the teacher had the student pick a spot to sit that they thought would help them be successful.	It worked sometimes and not others, but the student knew that the teacher was trying to help.
A student was struggling with journal writing. He would put his head on the table, refuse to write, and say, "I don't know what to write about!"	The teacher offered an alternative writing activity: responding to reading. He could write about how he felt about a book he'd read.	He enjoyed this so much more than journal writing and would smile as he wrote. He also wrote a lot, even writing in complete sentences.

engage in problem-solving conferences with your porcupines. Many are still just learning to trust you, and trying to have a meaningful conversation about a struggle they're having might push them away.

What Is a Problem-Solving Conference?

There are many different ways to hold a problem-solving conference (PSC) with a student. I have been particularly influenced by the work of

Ruth Charney (The Social Conference in *Teaching Children to Care*), Ross Greene (Collaborative & Proactive Solutions), and Jonathan Erwin (The Process for Positive Change in *The Classroom of Choice*). This is a collaborative process where, as much as possible, you help students take control of the challenge they're experiencing. Instead of lecturing them and telling them what to do, you ask lots of questions and try to understand the source of their challenge. Then you work together with students to try to come up with a realistic strategy or solution to try.

Here are the steps for a problem-solving conference and a bit of advice about each step.

Step 1: Find a good time and place for a chat. This should be at a time when you are both calm and where you can talk without being interrupted. There are a variety of times during the day when you might have a PSC. Especially if the topic of the conference isn't private or heated, you might be able to have one during an academic period. You are already meeting with students one on one for academic conferences. It's easy to slide in a social conference. You might hold a conference during lunch or another break period. You might have a student come into school a few minutes early or stay a few minutes late. You might have a colleague or administrator take your class for a few minutes. (This is something I've found school administrators very willing to do.) With the permission of a colleague (and with the understanding that you'd be happy to reciprocate), you might pull a student from another class during a planning period.

Step 2: Name the problem and see if the student is willing to talk about it. "Hey, Jared. The last week or so you've been really frustrated with your reading group. How about we chat for a few minutes and see if we can think of some ideas that might help?" State the problem in a kid-centric way ("You've been frustrated with your reading group") rather than a teacher-centric way ("You've been uncooperative with your reading group"). The point of the conference is for you to help them with their problem, not to get them to stop causing you a problem. If they don't want to talk, the conference stops. You can try again later, or continue to try reminders, redirections, consequences, or other strategies.

Step 3: Try to understand the problem from the student's perspective. "So what's going on during the reading group that's making things so hard? What's your perspective?" Invite the student to share their view about what's happening. This is so important! You won't be able to help them come up with a possible solution if you don't understand the problem from their perspective. Kids will often struggle with this. They'll either quickly move to blame others ("My group is stupid!") or shrug and say some version of "I don't know." It helps to ask probing questions:

- "What isn't working well with your group?"
- "Could it be that you have different ideas from your groupmates?"
- "When do things tend to break down?"
- "How does it feel for you when . . . ?"

Step 4: Generate ideas to try. Once you and your student have identified the problem ("I never get my way in the group"), work with them to generate a list of ideas they might try. Again, they will likely have a hard time with this. If they knew a solution, they'd have tried it already. Try suggesting strategies you have seen work for other kids. ("I had a student who had this same thing happening last year, and he tried . . .") Jot down ideas in student-centric terms. (*I could ask the group to try one of my ideas. I might let the group know how I feel. I might remind myself that in a group of four, my ideas often won't be the ones chosen. I might walk away from the group and take some breaths if I am getting mad. I might suggest a new way of choosing ideas—maybe pulling them from a hat.*) If ideas are hard to think of, consider pausing the conference so you both have time to think. Reconvene in a day or two and try again.

Step 5: Choose one idea to try. Once you and the student have generated some ideas, see if there are one or two that the student wants to try. As the teacher, you can say no to ideas that don't fit with the class rules. ("I know it would be nice if the group always had to try your ideas first, but that wouldn't be respectful of others, so that's not a good solution.") If needed, jot down a reminder note for the student or create a simple plan for them to follow so they remember the solution they chose. Let them know that if this one doesn't work, you two can meet for another conference to try again.

Sometimes a kid gets upset during the conference and they shut down. Sometimes the idea that you think is best is one the student won't agree to try. Sometimes there just doesn't seem to be a good idea to be had. That's fine. Just the fact that you took time out of your day to try to help your student with a challenge they're having, and that you did so in an empathetic—not blaming or preachy—way lets your student know you care. When PSCs are facilitated well, they're warm, demanding, supportive, and empowering. They can be great relationship builders even when they don't yield a productive outcome.

Step 6: Check in—soon. One of the ways you show commitment to your student and build trust with them is to follow up about how their solution is working. Set a reminder on your calendar so you don't forget. "Hey, Jared. How'd the last reading group go? Did you try asking the group for a new way to make decisions?" If their solution seems to be working, you might offer congratulations. If it's not, see if they want to have another conference to try thinking of some other ideas.

Who Should Lead Problem-Solving Conferences?

The adult who is with the student when they're having a hard time should be the one to run the problem-solving conference. I can't stress this enough: Don't outsource these conferences to other adults. You don't need a counseling degree to have one-on-one problem-solving conversations with a student. And because these PSCs are such great relationship-builders, you should be the one to facilitate them. In one middle school I worked in, the assistant principal told me that he has the best relationship with the 10 toughest kids in the school because he's the one who listens to them when they're upset. "I'm not the one who should have the best relationship with these kids," he told me. "I don't want kids wanting to come see me when they're having a hard time. . . . They should be going to see their teachers."

How Should You Ease into Problem-Solving Conferences?

Here are a few ideas for easing into this strategy so that you'll be able to use it effectively.

- **Teach PSCs to your class.** Consider introducing the idea of problem-solving conferences proactively and directly to your students. Let them know you're going to tell them about a strategy that you'll use throughout the year to help them solve individual challenges when they arise. Explain the purpose and steps of a problem-solving conference, and share some instances when it might come in handy (experiencing repeated writers block, playground/lunchroom problems, etc.). You could even get a student to act out a PSC with you in a fishbowl so that the class can watch one in action. Teaching PSCs to the whole class normalizes them and lets your porcupines know that they are a strategy for everyone.
- **Practice PSCs.** Like anything else, PSCs get easier and better the more you practice. This is a great time of year to try a few. I recommend practicing some "easy" ones. Try conferences with students

you already have a solid relationship with on problems that aren't emotionally charged. Later in the year, you may end up having some challenging PSCs. For example, you might have to navigate having a conference with a prickly student who is using racist insults to taunt a vulnerable peer. It will be hard to stay calm. The more you've practiced the steps and structures of a PSC, the more of your energy you can devote to maintaining a warm and supportive demeanor during an emotionally charged conference.

- **Plan logistics.** It can be helpful to jot down notes about each step of the PSC before you meet with the student. This can help you stay on track, especially as you're learning how to facilitate effective PSCs. Also think through when you will have PSCs throughout the year. Will you try the lunch block? Can you have them during class as students work independently? Will you have a colleague or administrator take your class for a few minutes? See Figure 9.2.

- **Try more challenging PSCs as you and your students are ready.** By the end of December, you may have built a strong enough relationship foundation to start using PSCs with even your most challenging porcupines. And remember, PSCs are one of the most powerful tools for building and strengthening positive relationships, so go ahead and give them a shot. If a student shuts down in the middle of the conference, you can always stop the conference and try again another time.

Once again, remember the power of the one-on-one problem-solving conference. Several of the ideas in the adjusting expectations chart in Figure 9.1 came from teachers sitting down with their students to talk about challenges they were having and to think of possible solutions. In some ways, this takes the pressure off you to be the one who must come up with all the ideas for adjusting expectations for your students. You can talk with your students and come up with ideas together. You can be demanding as you help kids do better through warm and collaborative conferences. By this point in the year, even your most challenging students should be ready to try problem-solving conferences with you.

And, once again, remember not to outsource these conversations to administrators or counselors. How could someone else possibly understand the particulars of the challenge that kids are struggling with if they're not in the room when the struggle is happening? And how would

FIGURE 9.2
Problem-Solving Conference Tool

1. **Find a good time and place for a chat.**
   * Adult and student are calm.
   * The environment is neutral or pleasant.
   * There is adequate time to talk.

2. **Name the problem and see if the student is willing to talk about it.**
   * Stay calm and neutral.
   * State the problem clearly.
   * Ask the student if they agree to work on the problem together. For example, "When things get rough on the playground, people can get hurt and the games aren't as fun. Is this something you think we could work on together?"
   * If the student won't work on the problem, the conference is done. Have a back-up plan ready, if possible.

3. **Try to understand the problem from the student's perspective.**
   * Ask questions to understand the student's perspective. For example, "Could it be . . . ?" "Is . . . happening?" "How does it feel for you when . . . ?"

4. **Generate ideas to try.**
   * Think of ideas together.
   * Try to come up with multiple possibilities.

5. **Choose one idea to try.**
   * The student chooses.
   * The teacher approves or agrees.
   * Create a simple plan together.
   * Decide on a follow-up time or date to officially check in.

6. **Check in—soon.**
   * Touch base early.
   * Follow up on agreed-upon time or date to confer.

---

someone else come up with an idea for adjusting expectations that you'd be fine with? What if, for example, a well-meaning adult tries to help a student who keeps disengaging from writing and getting disruptive. They suggest that the student take a walk and get a drink of water when they're struggling with writing. Leaving the room when they're struggling is probably the last thing this kid needs to do. Does this adjustment work for you?

Probably not. That's why you need to be the one to hold the problem-solving conference. If you want some help from the counselor or assistant principal, have them come in and monitor your other students as they write so you can have a quick conference with the one who's struggling.

Continuing to Build Relationships with Students

Throughout the fall, you've been taking notes about your students as you get to know them. You now know that Mark is into Minecraft and Venus likes Ariana Grande. That's a good start, but can you actually talk with students about those topics?

Of Pokémon and Boy Bands

Jordan was quirky. He rarely got angry or disruptive, but he would often shut down, retreating into his own little world. There was speculation that Jordan was on the autism spectrum, but his dad refused to have any testing done. The teacher he had the year before slipped into a distant relationship and would let him sit in the back of the room for long stretches of the day, drawing and writing fantasy stories. She may have avoided conflict with him, but he didn't participate in a lot of regular daily work. His stories were elaborate and deeply personal. He didn't really care if anyone else read them. Drawing and writing were his way of living them. I knew his inspiration for many of his stories were Pokémon cards and cartoons, content I did not find interesting. Still, I wanted to be able to talk with Jordan about his interest, so I forced myself to watch a few episodes several nights in a row.

I'm not going to say that I became a Pokémon fan. I didn't. But I was surprised at how much I found in common between those shows and some of my favorite fantasy and sci-fi stories such as *Star Wars* and *The Lord of the Rings*. Underdog heroes battled dark forces, overcoming seemingly insurmountable odds. Friends rescued friends. There was action, quick and compelling dialogue, and humor. I got it. And I found myself not only better able to talk with Jordan about his stories but also better able to understand why he liked them.

Kelsey was really into boy bands. When she stomped into the classroom in the morning and attacked me with, "You're talking about baseball again? The Red Sox are stooopid!" what she was really saying was, "You're always talking about things I don't care about. I wish you would talk about things I like!" So I worked at it. I'd ask her about a concert she said she was going to. (She was often talking about concerts she was going to. I'm not sure if she ever went.) I'd later look up the artist and listen to some of their music. Again, I didn't become a fan, but I could at least talk a little bit more intelligently about music that Kelsey liked, and she knew I was trying. I could see her smile, almost imperceptibly, when I told her I had listened to a song she liked.

What are some of your porcupines' interests? What music do they listen to? What sports do they follow? What video games do they play? Take some time to become familiar with some of their interests and weave these into your conversations with them. They'll appreciate your efforts.

Connect with Families

Another way to deepen connections with students is to continue to build connections with their families. The more you know your students' families and the more their families like and trust you, the better the year will be for everyone.

- **Hold conferences.** In many schools, November is parent–teacher conference time. You'll of course need to share some of your concerns about your porcupines with their families. Make sure, however, to also be ready to share lots of good things too. What are their strengths? What are some of their successes so far this year? What do you like about them?
- **Ask for advice, not a fix.** Sometimes when I was struggling with a student, I'd call home looking for help. "Hi, Mrs. Ackerman, it's Mr. Anderson. I'm calling looking for some advice. Macy has seemed really distracted lately. She's having a hard time keeping her mind on schoolwork and getting work completed. Are you seeing anything like that at home? Do you have any ideas for me—anything I might try?" Remember that parents and caregivers are the ones who know their children best. They can be great resources to tap into. On the other hand, be cautious about asking them to fix a school problem at home. A teacher once pointed out that they (the teacher) couldn't make a kid clean their bedroom any more than a parent could make a kid pay attention during a math lesson. As a parent, there just wasn't anything I could do when one of my kids was struggling to be flexible with a science group in middle school.
- **Know when not to call.** Sometimes it's better not to contact families. Maybe parents are going through a divorce, and they don't have head-space to handle school trouble. Perhaps there's been a death in the

family or some other catastrophe. There might be times it's better not to reach out to families at all. I found out in the middle of one year, from a guidance counselor in our school, that there was a rule at Bobby's house. If one kid got in trouble, they all got punished. And punishment was getting hit with a belt. If the 16-year-old broke curfew, all six kids, from the 16-year-old right down to the 6-year-old, lined up in the living room for the belt line. There was no way I was going to have Bobby and all his siblings whipped with a belt for Bobby getting into a scuffle with another kid on the playground. I could handle that myself.

Holding Students Accountable for Work and Learning

Teachers do students a disservice when they offer support but not empowerment or when they're warm but not demanding when it comes to academic work. Some porcupines seem exquisitely skilled at self-sabotage, and they need teachers to save them from themselves. They procrastinate and get behind in projects. They neglect to practice or study enough to become truly competent. They accept bad grades, seeming to not care. They struggle with delaying gratification and have a hard time doing uncomfortable or challenging things (like conjugating verbs or practicing an oral presentation) when there are easier and more enjoyable temptations nearby (friends to talk with or computers to play games on).

Part of this is developmental. While kids' brains are still cooking, they sometimes need us to be their surrogate prefrontal cortex. Some of this involves skill development. Students often don't have the skills they need to be successful with certain kinds of schoolwork. They might, for example, be asked to solve complex problems without anyone ever teaching them practical strategies for managing frustration. So they tune out or melt down because they don't know what else to do.

There might be any number of reasons that kids struggle to learn or complete work, so they need your support, but you should be careful not to over-support. There's a difference between scaffolding and enabling. This is why differentiation is so important. You can't expect kids to do work that's too hard. That's often when you end up giving too much help—because they really can't do it on their own. If the work has been differentiated so that it's in students' Goldilocks zones, you don't need to hold students' hands. Then it's reasonable for you to hold kids accountable for doing good work.

But how? It's so easy to say that you should "hold kids accountable," but what does that actually look like?

Strategies That Seem to Hold Kids Accountable but Actually Don't

First, let's explore a couple of common strategies that don't work. They offer the façade of accountability, but they don't lead to students getting work done or gaining competency.

- **Nagging.** "Jeremy, come on. You know you need to get going, or you're never going to have your writing ready for our deadline on Friday!" Jeremy nods, furrows his brow, and puts his head down. "I know! I'll get it done!" "Ellie, you really should put your independent reading book down and focus on your reading group book. You're meeting with your group tomorrow, and you're not ready." Ellie smiles and says, "Got it" but doesn't switch books. Reminders are important, and they're one way you can help keep kids on track. But when reminding turns into badgering and cajoling, you're not really holding kids accountable. They can simply ignore your pleas and not get work done.

- **Bribing.** "If you can read one more page, you'll earn a sticker on your sticker chart!" "If you check off all the items on the rubric, you'll earn at least an 80. If you do extra work, you can get bonus points." "If you work extra hard this week, we'll watch a movie on Friday!" These kinds of extrinsic motivators sometimes work in the short term, but a wide body of research has shown that they often decrease student motivation and learning in the long run (Anderson, 2021; Deci et al., 1999; Kohn, 2018). It might feel like you're holding kids accountable by giving them extra incentive to complete work or learn content, but the inherent problem in these systems is that you're implying that the work is optional. You make learning into a transaction that kids can opt out of. All students need to do is decide that they don't care about a sticker or points or movies, and they can decline your offer.

- **Failing.** When my son was in middle school, he got hopelessly behind in his ELA class one year. He was a phenomenal reader and writer, but time management challenges and the inability to delay gratification made it hard for him to complete schoolwork he didn't want to do. After a few late assignments piled up, he got overwhelmed. It was like what happened when his bedroom got so messy that he couldn't even start cleaning it—it was just too much. My wife and I had a conference with his teacher. She was confused and a bit exasperated. "He's getting an *F*," she said. "He doesn't seem to care!" Of course he cared, but the prospect of getting an *F* was only fueling his sense of desperation and incompetence and made it harder to find good energy for work. Have you seen this happen in your school? Kids who you know are more than capable of good work are allowed to fail. You say you're "holding kids accountable" by giving them bad grades, but where's the accountability if they're still not learning or getting their work done?

- **Grading a group.** You may assign a group project and let the kids know they're all in this together, so they'll be graded as a team. You hope students will hold each other accountable, but instead, one or two kids resentfully carry the group, unwilling to get a bad grade. Others don't (or can't) do their fair share. This is bad for everyone, but it's especially damaging for our porcupines.

- **Grade retention.** This is a strategy I sometimes hear talked about wistfully by some high school educators. "There's too much social promotion in this district," they state. "If kids can't read at grade level, they should be held back. Then maybe they'd catch up." There just isn't evidence to support this practice. In fact, John Hattie's meta-analysis work revealed major problems with it: "This is one of the few areas in education where it is difficult to find any studies with a positive ($d > 0.0$) effect, and the few that do exist still hover close to a zero effect. . . . Retention has been found to have a negative effect on academic achievement in language arts, reading, mathematics, work-study skills, social studies, and grade point average. Promoted students score better than retained students on social and emotional adjustment, and behavior, self-concept, and attitude toward school" (2009, p. 97). Retaining a student doesn't hold them accountable. It dramatically increases their chances of struggling in school even more.

Now let's explore some ideas that might help you be more effectively demanding. I use the word "might" intentionally, for in the end, if a kid really decides to buckle down and not learn, I'm not sure you can really force them. But there are some strategies to try that give students a better chance of being successful.

Require Extra Time

If students aren't making good use of class time, you might schedule another time for them to come in and get caught up. This often requires teachers to put in some extra time and effort, but how can you expect students to go above and beyond if you aren't willing to do the same? Here are a few times to consider.

- **Before or after school.** As a classroom teacher, I got to school early. It was my best time to work, especially when my own children were young, as I needed to get home early in the afternoon to take care of them. When I had students who needed extra time, I'd contact their caregivers to see if they could be dropped off early. If you tend to get schoolwork done in the afternoon, schedule make-up times then.
- **WIN time.** If you have a block of the day designed for extra help and extensions (often called WIN: What I Need), make sure to use it. Require students to meet with you during this block to catch up.
- **Middle of the day.** Be cautious about requiring students to miss their lunch or recess time. Teachers are often guaranteed a duty-free lunch for a reason. A break in the middle of the day is an important reset, and often porcupines are the ones who most need to reconnect with peers and get outside and run. Still, you might use this time occasionally, or you might offer it as an option to a student.
- **Schedule an extra work period.** Especially if you have many students who are behind in work, you might schedule a period or two as an extra work block for the whole class. Provide some engaging and relevant extension or practice options for kids who are caught up and require students who are behind to work on assigned tasks.
- **Have students help create the catch-up plan.** Another way to balance support and empowerment with students who are behind in work is to have them cocreate the catch-up plan with you. They might set their own new deadline for completing work or create a checklist for the small steps they need to take along the way. Offering students some autonomy can help them follow through while also gaining new skills and strategies for the next time they are falling behind.

The tone and feeling of these extra times are important. On the one hand, you want them to be warm and supportive—letting students know that you're there to help. On the other hand, you don't want it to be *too* enjoyable, especially for students who are making up work because they aren't getting it done when they should. When I had students come in before school, I made sure I was busy with quiet work so that students couldn't chit-chat once their assigned work was done. I didn't want them to *want* to come in before school.

If these times are too supportive, they may enable learned helplessness. You don't want students to figure that it's fine not to work during class time because they can come in during WIN time to get things done.

You also don't want this consequence—having to make up work outside of class time—to feel too harsh. It's going to feel like a punishment if you intentionally take time away from what kids most love (recess, soccer practice, etc.) just to make a point. The tone you use can help you thread this needle. If you layer on shame and guilt or emphasize how kids are losing free time or missing soccer practice because they were irresponsible ("See? That's what happens when you're irresponsible! You miss soccer practice!"), kids can now be angry with and resentful of you. Instead, try for a tone of empathy. ("It stinks that you're missing soccer practice right now. See how much you can get done so that you're caught up and can go tomorrow.") This increases the chances that kids will be frustrated with their own behavior and work to correct it—instead of blaming you for being mean.

The strategy of having kids make up work outside of class time is something you should use sparingly. Especially during the beginning of the school year, it helps set a tone of accountability that can help kids get into more productive habits. If some students are struggling over and over to get work completed, try having a problem-solving conference to uncover the source of the problem. There's likely something getting in their way. The work might be too difficult. There might be a challenging social dynamic going on that you're unaware of. The student might need some extra coaching around self-management strategies.

Use Grades That Reflect Learning and Require Competence

One of the problems with traditional grades is that they make work and learning transactional. When teachers say to students, "If you don't do your work, you'll get a bad grade," they're essentially saying, "It's fine to not do your work. You can just take a zero." For kids who struggle with regulation, who have a hard time making themselves do hard things, or who have received lots of bad grades in the past, this is an easy out. My daughter has a friend who was reluctant to study for tests. She thought that if she studied and got a bad grade, she would have wasted her time. For her, the only reason to study was to get a grade, not to learn content. This is a common mindset in students.

Let's explore a few grading practices that are less likely to lead students to taking the easy way out and more likely to encourage them to engage in learning.

- **Competency-based grading.** There has been much written about moving to competency-based grading, and it's beyond the scope of this book to get into it in detail. The basic idea is that grades should reflect what students have learned, not how many points they have accumulated. Teachers look for evidence of competency through a variety of mechanisms including daily work, conferences, observations, and more formal assessments. Students can't receive "semester killer" zeros for missing work and don't get underwater with a series of bad grades that makes trying to improve their average an effort in futility. They also can't get bonus points for bringing in canned goods or participating in class discussions. Competency-based grading is good for all students, but porcupines are often the ones who most suffer in traditional grading systems. There are many great resources available about competency-based grading. I highly recommend Chapter 14 of *Building Thinking Classrooms in Mathematics, Grades K–12* by Peter Liljedahl (2021).
- **Pass-fail grading.** My daughter is just beginning the next phase of her academic career to become a doctor of veterinary medicine. One program that she considered uses only pass-fail grading, and she found this appealing. It takes a lot of pressure off worrying about whether you got an 89 or a 91 on a test. Students aren't ranked against each other, and they don't have GPAs. The goal isn't to beat other students—it's to learn enough information to become a successful veterinarian. To pass, students need a score of at least 80 percent on assessments. (Notice that here "passing" is not a *D-*, which is a low bar, it's a *B-*.) If they don't get that, they need to go back and relearn and try again. This kind of grading system is incredibly demanding as it *requires* learning. The old (discouraging) adage that *"Ds* get degrees" doesn't fly in a pass-fail system.
- ***A, B,* or not yet.** Here's another version of pass-fail grading, shared by Daniel Venables (2020). A high school teacher known for his ability to teach 9th graders to write uses a simple grading system. Any piece

of work receives a grade of *A* or *B*. If it receives a grade of "not yet," it has to be reworked, incorporating suggestions from the teacher, and resubmitted. The work is not complete until it has received an *A* or *B*. There is no room in this classroom for *C*s, *D*s, or *F*s. Everyone must achieve at high levels.

- **Convert competency-based grades to traditional ones.** I've worked in several schools where individual teachers want to move to competency-based practices even though their school continues to use traditional grades. It's possible! You can support your porcupines through more effective grading practices and still play ball with your school and district. One middle school math teacher used a simple conversion after an assessment. There were four competencies being assessed. If a student was fully competent in all four, they received an *A*. If they were fully competent in three and partially in one, they received an *A*- and so on.

- **Redos and retakes.** Have you heard some version of this joke? Q: *What do they call people who take five times to pass the bar exam?* A: *Lawyers.* In the "real world" there are tons of instances where people are given unlimited chances to pass high-stakes assessments. People can take LSATs, bar exams, SATs, and CPA exams over and over. What if we cooked redos and retakes into our systems? Cristin Kochanowicz, a French teacher in Cheshire, Connecticut, was looking for a way to help students truly learn what they needed to learn so that they could continue to progress in French as they got older (2023). She decided to try requiring students to retake sections of quizzes if they hadn't learned enough. She found that this required some more work upfront, and she was initially worried that she was creating too much work for herself. However, once students realized they were actually being held accountable for learning, they started studying more and needed to retake portions of quizzes less. She came to realize that a systematic process for retakes actually raised the bar for learning in her classes.

Actively Supervise

By this point in the school year, many routines and procedures are running on autopilot. Kids know how to enter the classroom and get settled. They understand expectations in the lunchroom and playground. They've been to several assemblies and all-school gatherings, and they've done pretty well. It's so tempting to start to relax supervision. You're on playground or lunchroom duty, and you want to take a few minutes to catch up with a colleague, asking about their weekend or about their plans for the holidays. You tell the class to head down to the assembly on their own so you can use the restroom or check in with someone in the office. Shouldn't the class be able to handle these things by now?

Maybe. Maybe not. As energy and anxiety build around the holiday season, students might need a bit more active supervision now than they did a few weeks ago. Some porcupines might be on the edge of fight, flight, or freeze even more often than normal. They need you to continue to be demanding in your expectations, and you can't do that if you're not watching them and supporting them as needed. You may accidentally be setting your porcupines up for failure if you loosen supervision during this time of year.

Avoid Character Judgments

By November and December, some of your porcupines' struggles and behaviors may be accumulating for you. It can be so easy to let this spill over in sarcasm, snark, or shaming.

- "John! We've been talking about this all year long! When are you going to finally get it?"
- "Oh, that's *real* mature, Maria. You're in high school. What are you, 5 years old?"
- "I can't take it anymore, Jamal. Your laziness is driving me crazy!"

We've all been there. We've said something we shouldn't. If (when) you mess up, you should apologize and work to be better. When reminding and redirecting, instead of sliding into character judgments, let's remember to address what the kid has done, not who the kid is.

- "John. I know you're excited to share, but you need to raise your hand."
- "Maria, I can see that you're frustrated. Take a few deep breaths and try talking to me again in a polite voice."
- "Jamal, you can do better work than that. Head back to your seat and keep working."

Considering What You're Celebrating

Finally, let's consider a few ideas about handling the actual holidays with your students. Belonging is one of the most important intrinsic motivators, or psychological needs, that humans have. With this in mind, let's think of how you can keep celebrations inclusive of all students.

I celebrate Christmas with my family. It's my favorite holiday. I love getting the biggest possible tree that will fit in our living room and eagerly count down the days to the 25th. However, when I was in the classroom in a public school, I didn't think it was my place to bring my personal holidays (especially ones with religious connections) into my classroom. Over the years, I had students whose families were Christian, Jewish, Muslim, atheist, agnostic, Jehovah's Witness, Wicca, and many more. I was in a school, however, where many teachers did celebrate Christmas in their classrooms, and I didn't want my students to be the only ones not having a party. Fortunately, there are plenty of fun ways to celebrate with your students this time of year—ones that are inclusive of all students.

Hold a Solstice Celebration

Consider celebrating the winter solstice—a moment that has been revered and celebrated by humans for eons. You might have students share some of what they love about this time of year or the coming winter. You might host a luncheon in the classroom where students bring in favorite dishes from their families. One year I did this, and kids had so much fun trying Jamaican jerk chicken, Vietnamese rice milk, and a variety of other family favorites. Interestingly, this particular class celebration had more families join in than most others that I tried.

Celebrate Learning

Do you have a big unit that's coming to an end? How about hosting a celebration-of-learning event? Have students put on a showcase to teach others about the unit. They might reorganize and decorate the room and have other classes stream through. You might invite families to an in-school or after-school event where students can show off what they've learned. This event can boost students' sense of purpose as they learn—knowing they're going to have a sharing event—while also serving as a community-building event for students and the school community.

Invite Your Students to Share

Although you might not actively celebrate holidays in a classroom, that doesn't mean you should neglect that part of kids' lives. Far from it! You might invite students to share their families' traditions and celebrations during morning or advisory meetings. I learned so much about my students and their families in this way, and it was a great way to help kids get to know each other as well.

As always, keep your most vulnerable students in mind as you structure these sharings. Keep topics and questions you pose inclusive so that all kids can participate positively.

A Look Ahead: January Is Re-Month

When kids come back from the holiday break, they'll need some time to get back into the flow of the school year. In some ways, January can be almost like a mini version of the first weeks of school. That's what we'll explore in the next chapter. For now, you can start thinking ahead about some of the things you might need to review with students to help them get back into school mode after the vacation.

January Is Re-Month

January

It was January 2, and students were heading back through the front doors to school. I had worked with the faculty at this school many times, but this was my first time at the school when kids were present. I was looking forward to observing in classrooms and teaching some lessons later in the day. Teachers greeted students cheerfully as they walked through the doors. "Hey, Christina! It's good to see you! Welcome back, Mohammed. How was vacation?" Some kids smiled and waved. A few stopped for a high five or fist bump. But most looked lethargic or exhausted. Some didn't even look up as they were greeted. They could have been auditioning for a bit part in *Night of the Living Dead.*

When kids come back from winter break, you may be tempted to dive right back into school, as if you were just away for a long weekend. This isn't what kids need, and your porcupines in particular may crash and burn if you go too quickly in the first few days back. Kids' sleep schedules have been all over the place, and they've been away from school and out of their normal routines. They've probably eaten lots of junk food and had very different expectations for behavior and language. For some, the holidays were full of angst and stress. They need help easing back into school. In some ways, the first week back is almost a mini version of the first few weeks of school.

Years ago, I read a blog post in which a teacher called January "Re-Month." I've searched everywhere for the post and author to no avail. Too bad— I wish I could give credit where credit is due, for this simple phrase captures the importance of January. It's the time to revisit rules and routines, reestablish expectations, and reconnect with students and help them reconnect with each other.

Before you read on, there's an important idea to consider if you're a high school teacher or a special area teacher who gets whole new classes at the beginning of January. If you get brand new groups of kids for second semester, you'll need to do more than just reteach, reconnect, and revisit. You'll need to begin all over again. Consider going back to Chapter 7 to remember how to create rules with a group, establish routines, and begin to build connections and relationships.

Revisiting Routines

Remember all the time and energy you spent in the fall teaching routines and helping students become more independent with them? This was important for all students but especially for your porcupines. Students who struggle with regulation and relationships often rely on routines. Knowing how the classroom works gives them a much-needed sense of predictability, helping them feel safer in school.

In addition to helping reestablish a smooth and efficient classroom, there are a couple of other benefits to revisiting routines in early January. For students who had little structure or supervision over vacation, this is a chance for them to recalibrate and get back into school mode. It also gives you a chance to reestablish your authority as the leader of the classroom. Remember that students may have lost some school stamina over vacation, and many are certainly tired. Reviewing routines gives you a chance to slide back into school gently, helping students catch their breath before diving full-on into projects and complex work. Here are some suggestions and strategies for revisiting routines (Anderson, 2016b).

Suggestions for Revisiting Routines

- **Be proactive.** Think ahead about the most important routines students need to remember so that the first few days run smoothly. Revisit these routines before (or just as) they're needed.
- **Be clear about purpose.** Following routines shouldn't be an exercise in compliance for students. Make sure to remind students *why* each routine is important. ("Walking quietly in the halls allows other classes to stay focused." "Making eye contact while conferring in writing helps you listen well and show respect for your partner.")

- **Don't overdo it.** Use the various strategies listed below to give students just the right amount of revisiting—enough so they can be successful but not too much that they feel bored or condescended to.
- **Observe your students.** Don't worry if you don't anticipate every routine that might need attention. Watch your students, and you'll quickly see which ones you missed.

Strategies for Revisiting Routines

- **Elicit ideas from students.** "Who can remember the routine we have for getting my attention when you have a question or comment?" A simple question like this is likely all students need to remember some of the simplest and most straightforward routines.
- **Model.** If seeing a positive model of a behavior or routine might be helpful, give a brief demonstration or ask a student to give one. "Let's remember how we join in the circle for a reading lesson. Who can show us what that looks like?"
- **Ask for revisions.** Were there some routines that weren't working well? If so, ask the class for ideas about ways to adjust. "I remember that our routine for putting away devices was a bit bumpy before vacation. Who has an idea for how we might make it better?"

Revisiting Rules

You might also want to revisit classroom or school rules when you come back to school after the winter break. You might do this through a few short whole-class meetings. If your class is dysregulated as a group, you could have students answer questionnaires and surveys or meet with you in small groups. Whatever format you use, this is time well spent. Remember that rules and norms at home are often very different from ones at school, and kids will need to get back into school-rule mode when they come back. Here are a few ideas for how to revisit rules.

Remind Students About the Rules

You might facilitate a class discussion, a small-group meeting, or have a one-on-one chat with students you work with. Make sure your tone is open and invitational, not accusatory or exasperated. Remember that you want students to see rules as positive goals you're all working toward—to create the kind of environment that will lead to great learning.

Here are some open-ended questions you might use or adapt to kick off the discussion.

- "Think back to December. Which rule(s) do you think we/you were especially good at living up to? Which one(s) were especially challenging to live up to? Were there certain times of day or places in the building where it was especially easy or hard to follow some of our rules?"
- "Which of our rules do you think is most helpful as we continue to create a safe and engaging learning environment?"
- "In the next few weeks, we'll be digging into [share about an upcoming unit]. Which rules might be especially helpful as we get into that work?"

Adjust Rules

Perhaps the wording of a rule didn't quite match what was actually happening in the classroom. During a class meeting, ask students for suggestions about modifications to the rules of the class. This will refresh their sense of autonomy while also reinforcing the importance of rules to guide behavior and work. Reworking your rules can give them fresh life and energy.

Re-create Rules

If your whole group needs a full reset, you might want to go through a mini version of the rule creation process you used back in the fall. This might be an especially good idea if you feel like some of the rules you created aren't working at all. Have students consider goals for the second half of the year, envision an ideal learning environment, generate some possible rules, narrow them down to a few, and check for consensus and agreement. Post them in easily visible spots, and remember to refer to them often.

Remember to Use the Language of the Rules

Regardless of how you revisit rules in January, this is a great time to check in on how you're talking about them. If you're at all like me, you were really good about this early in the fall. Right after you created or introduced rules to students, you remembered to frame positive behavior and expectations in ways that connected with and reinforced rules. ("Hey, everyone. We're about to have another partner chat. Remember our rule about being respectful. Make sure to give your partner your attention. Remember to 'share the air' and both take turns talking.") Then, as the school year progressed, you forgot to mention the rules as often. The rules poster fell off the wall or got covered with another display, and you barely noticed.

This is a great time of year to get back on track. Remember that when you use the language of the rules instead of your own personal expectation as the reason for hard work or kind behavior, you reinforce the power of the class's expectations and reduce getting into power struggles. See Figure 10.1 for a quick reminder.

FIGURE 10.1

Frame Expectations Through Rules

Instead of Framing Expectations Through Your Own Voice . . .	Frame Expectations Through the Language of Class Rules
"I need you to work really hard on this next project."	"Remember our class goal of putting in 'strong effort'? This project is going to definitely require some of that!"
"I want everyone to settle down and listen to me so I can give you directions for our next activity!"	"Hey, everyone. It's time to work at our rule of listening respectfully. That will help you hear the directions for our next activity!"
"It's important to me that you collaborate well in your group. How can you do that?"	"How can you work at our class norm of 'take care of others' as you collaborate in your group?"
"I expect you all to be safe when we head out to the playground for recess."	"Remember to be safe (our first class rule!) when we head out to the playground for recess."

Avoid Asking Students "Did You Make a Good Choice?"

When a student has broken a rule, a common practice in many schools is to ask the student some version of "Was that a good choice?"

Imagine yourself as a kid who has been in an argument with another kid. They said something mean, and you shot back with something meaner. The teacher heard what you said and is talking with you about it. You're still upset, and now you're even more mad because you're the one getting in trouble. Also imagine that you are fiercely independent and can't stand it when people take away your power. "Mike, was that a good choice to call your friend a mean name?" the teacher asks. How might you react?

What if you thought it *was* a good choice? What if one of your parents tells you that if a kid pushes you around, you need to stand up for yourself and fight back? What if your friend said something really mean, and you're still hurt?

Or what if you didn't think at all? The mean comment just came out. The question, "Did you make a good choice?" implies intentionality. It says that kids made a rational decision—a choice—when doing the thing they shouldn't have. (*Hmmm. My friend just called me a mean name. I can either take a deep breath and think about a respectful response, or I can yell a mean thing back. What are the pros and cons of each of these choices? I guess I'll say something mean.*)

Of course, teachers use this phrase with good intentions. You're trying to reinforce the idea that kids have the power to make good choices or remind them of their autonomy. But in this moment, there's only one acceptable answer to this question. Kids are supposed to hang their heads, drop their eyes, and submit: "No."

This is another way you might accidentally set porcupines up for a power struggle: to accuse them of being intentionally thoughtless and to ask them to be submissive—to admit they were wrong. It's no surprise that some kids shut down and refuse to answer this question or flare up and yell, "Yeah! He was being a jerk!"

What could you say instead? First, don't ask a question that's not really a question. In the heat of the moment, when tempers are still hot, you might say, "Mike, I know you were upset, but it's not all right to call people names like that." This would be a great time to reconnect with your rules: "Mike, what you just said doesn't fit with our class rule about being respectful." These kinds of short, clear statements remind students (those involved and those nearby) that you will continue to be demanding in service of safety and upholding the classroom rules.

Later, when tempers have cooled, you might have a problem-solving conference with the student to help them think ahead about what else they could do the next time something like this happens. Or you might pull the two kids aside together for a quick chat to try to sort out what happened and to think about how to handle things in accord with your class rules the next time.

Revisiting Consequences

Just as kids need a reset about routine and rules, they can also use a reminder about consequences. Discipline was likely very different at home over the break. It might have been overly harsh, or it might have felt like there weren't any rules or consequences at all.

Have a short class meeting or two to review how consequences work at school. You could do this as a part of revisiting the rules. Give a few examples of common behavior mistakes and have students share some simple logical consequences. Remember to keep a matter-of-fact tone ("We all make mistakes") as opposed to a threatening one ("You'd better not screw up"). This is another great chance to set a tone of being warm and demanding.

Help Students See Positive Consequences

An interesting thought exercise to try with students at this point in the year is to help them see that both natural and logical consequences can be positive as well as negative. A positive natural consequence of students playing fairly or working cooperatively with others is that others want to play and work with them more. A logical consequence of students showing greater responsibility when leaving the classroom for bathroom breaks or to run errands is that they gain more trust and are given more freedom.

Again, you might generate a few examples, share those with the class, and talk about possible natural and logical consequences. Remember that these kinds of conversations are good for all students, and it's especially important for your porcupines to see these as normal class discussion topics. This helps them understand that you're warm and demanding with *all* students.

Be Careful with This Consequence

Let's say a student is fooling around with a snack. Maybe they're throwing a bag of chips up and catching it over and over. It's making a lot of noise and distracting others. A logical consequence might be to take the student's snack away. If they can't handle the privilege of having a snack, they should lose it. However, there's a caution to consider here.

Be careful about taking anything away from kids permanently. Even if they're playing with a cheap junky toy, I don't think we have the right to take the toy and never give it back. You might save it for the end of the day or even, depending on the situation, require a parent or guardian to reclaim an item.

Food is even more sensitive. For kids experiencing food insecurity, taking food away can elicit a full-on panic attack. At the same time, you shouldn't let a kid keep distracting others with a bag of chips. So you might have the student put their snack away for a while, either in their backpack or on a shelf in the classroom where they can see it and know it's not going away. Make sure to give the student a specific time they'll get it back, so they know they're not going to lose their food.

Rebuilding Stamina

Students will be tired when they come back from break, not refreshed. They're also out of shape when it comes to school. Kids who could read for 30 minutes straight in December might only be able to handle 15 or 20 in early January. Your class that could pay attention to a 10-minute direct teaching lesson before the break might fade after 5 minutes. Your porcupine who made so much social and academic progress in the late fall might seem like they're right back at square one.

Keep this in mind as you get back into academic work in January. Adjust direct teaching lessons as needed, perhaps breaking them into two parts with activities in between. Break large periods into smaller chunks. Provide more energizers, movement, and chances for active practice. You might also build in a few short breaks where kids can relax and chat before reengaging in work. Take the next few days to gradually build back up to where you were before the holidays, and kids will be back in school shape in a few days.

Reconnecting

You worked hard in the first months of school to build positive relationships with your students. You've also been working at helping kids make connections with each other so they can better work together. Make sure to take some time after the winter holiday break to reconnect with your students.

Conduct Check-Ins

Check in with your porcupines (and all students for that matter) when they return after the break. Greet kids at the door with a smile, use their names, and let them know you're glad to see them. Don't be surprised if kids seem subdued or out of sorts.

You can also touch base with kids throughout the day. As students are working on independent academic work and you're circulating and supporting, you can also check in with a few kids quietly. "Hey, Sophia. How was break?" "Good morning, James. Did you visit with your grandparents over the holiday?" Even just these small moments of touching base remind kids that you care about them.

Encourage Students to Share During Advisory and Morning Meetings

Structure a few activities where kids get to share some of what they did over the holiday break. I strongly encourage you not to let kids share what presents they got, as this can quickly lead to an unintentional brag-fest where kids feel resentful of classmates who got better stuff. Instead, have kids share stories. You might, for example, try a speed-dating style sharing structure where kids have several one- to two-minute chats with different partners each round. Give a thoughtful and structured prompt for each round. Students might share about someone they spent time with over the break in round one. In the next round, they might share something fun they did. In subsequent rounds, they could share foods they ate, games they played, shows they watched, or any other simple and inclusive topic. As you consider good topics, think about ones you know your porcupines can answer well, and as kids share, keep an ear out for what your porcupines share about—both to learn about how their break was and to manage things if their sharing starts to get inappropriate.

Getting a New Porcupine Mid-Year

Carlos came into my class mid-year. I'd heard he'd left his previous school in grand style: spray painting the f-word on a bench on the playground. His first couple of days, he was as sweet as pie and almost too polite. I was nervous. The third day, he arrived with a binder of baseball cards to share at morning meeting. I didn't usually let kids share stuff, but this seemed like a safe and concrete way for him to try sharing for the first time, so I said sure. Besides, how much tamer and safer can you get than baseball cards? (Right!?)

Here was how he shared: "Hey, everyone," he began, holding up his binder. "Today I wanted to share my baseball cards with you." He began to turn pages, one after the other. Kids leaned forward trying to see. "These cards are really important to me because my father gave them to me." He paused to turn a page, then continued. "He gave them to me right before he went to prison. He went to prison for doing something *really* bad." Kids cocked their heads to the side, and I jumped in. "All right, Carlos. Thanks for sharing this morning." I turned and looked at the class. "Carlos will take a few questions and comments now, *but just about the baseball cards.*" I looked hard at the other students. They got the idea and asked a couple of polite questions about the cards.

After the meeting, I pulled Carlos aside. "Before you share anything more at school about what's going on with your dad, I want you to check with your mom and see what you can share at school." He looked genuinely puzzled and responded, "All right, Mr. Anderson."

The next morning, I greeted him at the door first thing. "Hey, Carlos! It's good to see you this morning! Did you check with your mom about what you're allowed to share about your dad?" He nodded solemnly and said, "Yeah. She said I'm not supposed to talk about that at school." "Got it, thanks for checking," I responded.

Carlos, by the way, had a great rest of the year. He dropped the over-politeness after a few days but never had any serious trouble.

New students can show up at any time of year, but right after the holiday season seems to be a common one. It might be that parents' work changes around January 1. Or perhaps families try to time their move with the start of a new semester or right after a vacation so that they have time to move and kids get to join their new school at what feels like a fresh start.

It's not uncommon, however, for kids joining your class in the middle of the year to be experiencing a lot of instability in their lives. They could be immigrating from another country, experiencing a family break-up, or having some other major life upheaval.

It's unsettling and even scary to move to a new school, learn new routines, and establish new peer connections. Even for kids who aren't normally dysregulated and who aren't dealing with ongoing instability or acute stress outside of school, a move is tough. For kids whose lives are already tumultuous, it's of course that much harder.

You also know how one new student can often change the feel of a whole class. The more proactive and positive you are as you help a new student join the classroom community, the more likely it is that a new student will bring new life and energy to a room instead of more dysregulation.

Here are a few things you can do to prepare for a new student who shows up mid-year, whether they're a porcupine or not. These things will help any new student adjust more positively.

Give Off Positive Vibes When They Arrive

You might be surprised when a new student shows up at your door. Ideally, you'll know they're coming ahead of time, but sometimes, like with James (who I shared about in Chapter 1), they just appear. Plan for how you'll react when they arrive. Imagine how dispiriting it would be to be a new student walking into class on your first day in a new school and to have your new teacher react with annoyance or frustration at your arrival ("Oh, good grief, no one told me I was getting a new kid!"). Instead, be ready to react with delight ("Wow, I'm so excited you're here!"). Again, you never get a second chance at a first impression. Be ready to be warm and welcoming even if caught off guard. If you have an extra seat and a set of materials ready to go (as suggested in Chapter 6), you'll be even more ready to be calm and steady as you help welcome them to your class.

Adjust Your Advisory and Morning Meetings

The day a new student shows up, make sure to adjust your morning meeting or advisory period accordingly. It might be tempting to have them introduce themselves to the group, and perhaps an unusually self-assured student might feel comfortable doing this. My recommendation, however, is to let your new student choose how much they'd like to participate. Do they want to observe for a couple of days? Do they want to participate in parts but not all of this time?

You might also want to go with a simpler and safer version of advisory or morning meetings than you would normally have in January. Go back to a structure you might have used in the first weeks of school, so your new student can see a meeting that's not overwhelming. You could have your group introduce themselves to your new student, saying their name and something they like to do, but even this might feel overwhelming. Remember that you have the rest of the year to help your student get comfortable. Err on the side of safety.

Pair Them with a Student Guide

Another way to set a new student up for success is to pair them up with another student who can help them navigate the school during their first few days. Especially once the year is well underway, it can be easy to forget all the little routines that are now automatic for most kids: how to sign up for lunch, when it's all right to get up and move around the room, where supplies are kept, how the lunchroom works, and so on.

Pick someone you know will be kind and welcoming but is also strong and self-assured enough to handle themselves if your new student ends up being a bit prickly. In a self-contained elementary school setting, you might assign one or two students as your new student's go-to peers. In a middle or high school setting, have one student in your class who sits near the new student be the one to offer help.

Ease into Academics

Just as you might allow your new student to ease into your morning meeting or advisory group, it might be helpful to let them ease into academics.

Let them know they can spend the first few days observing. If they want to jump right in, great! But this might be overwhelming, especially if they've landed in the middle of a big collaborative project.

There's an important benefit to this if your new student does happen to be a porcupine. As they're observing other students at work, you can be observing them without trying to manage how they're interacting or handling tough academics. You can slowly get to know them and start to figure out who they might best work with and what they can (and can't) handle.

Introducing New Academic Structures

January isn't just about reviewing and revisiting. This is also a great time of year to introduce and try new learning structures—ones that build on your students' increasing skills and offer some fun new variety to learning. For example, a high school class might try Socratic seminars for the first time to give students a more authentic and dynamic way to discuss ideas. Or an elementary classroom might start book clubs as a part of a historical fiction literacy and social studies unit.

These new academic structures can breathe life into a learning community, but they can also elicit panic from porcupines. If you have students who get easily overwhelmed (and then melt down), think of ways you can help ease them into these new structures. One idea is to pull them aside for a quick preview to let them know what's coming. "Hey, Laura. We're trying a new academic activity later today, and I know you like to know what's coming. Would you like to hear a bit about it before I teach it to the class?" Or if you're going to need some volunteers to help role play the new structure in a fishbowl, you might invite students who need more preparation to be part of the role play team. That way, they can learn about the new structure and even practice it before it's time to try it for real in the classroom.

Even just a little bit of extra proactive preview work can help your porcupines better handle new academic structures so they can be successful.

Protecting Porcupines from Other Staff

As the school year wears on, some staff get worn down. Holiday stress doesn't only affect students. Some faculty come back from the holiday break just as exhausted as students. Unfortunately, sometimes when adults are exhausted and stressed out, they lose their cool more easily with porcupines. Some adults don't have the self-regulation or skills of empathy and caring that the most prickly students require. You may need to keep your eyes out for this and be ready to support your students—and even protect them if needed.

A story comes to mind. It was a chilly mid-year day, and I was on recess duty. One of my students, Bobby, asked if I wanted to throw a football around.

Bobby was definitely a porcupine. He came into 3rd grade with a reputation as a tough kid—one who could be belligerent, be defiant, and even engage in bullying. He was large for the grade and came from a tough family. He was the one who was lined up in the belt line with his siblings if any one kid got in trouble.

Bobby also had some incredible strengths. He was a strong reader and writer. He wrote a poem that year about fishing under the moonlight with his dad that blew me away. He also had a strong sense of justice. He bristled at anything that felt unfair. He just couldn't control his temper, so he sometimes violated his own moral code, which infuriated him even more. I looped with that class, so I had Bobby for two years, and I absolutely loved him. His defiant combative behaviors were few and far between—at least when I was with him. With other adults, it could be a different story.

Because he had a negative reputation (remember that he's only in 3rd grade at this point), some adults watched him like a hawk—pouncing on the smallest opportunity to reprimand him. If he was one of four kids jostling in line in the cafeteria, he would be the one who was called out. "Bobby! Keep your hands to yourself!" He also had a tougher time with adults he didn't know well. His inclination (which made sense given his abusive home life) was to not trust adults at first. It was common for him to struggle in special area classrooms and with substitute teachers. It was on this chilly mid-year day that a substitute teacher was mean-spirited, and I needed to intervene.

I asked Bobby to head to the gymnasium to borrow a football from the PE teacher so we could have a catch during recess. Bobby half-ran, half-skipped back into the building. A few minutes later, he reemerged, plodding with his head hung low. His eyes were heavy with tears. "What's up, Bobby? Was Mr. Rahn not there?" I asked.

Bobby choked a response. "No. It was Mr. Smith, the sub."

"Oh, well, where's the football?"

Bobby's eyes stayed glued to the ground. Through clenched teeth and tears he said, "Mr. Smith wouldn't give me one. He said he had told me there would be a day when I would need him for somethin'."

I knew Mr. Smith. He had worked with my students before, and I knew he could be brusque. This seemed more than harsh though. It was vindictive. Was he actually taking revenge on an 8-year-old for a misbehavior that had happened weeks or months ago? I let Bobby know that I'd be right back.

After motioning to the other teacher on duty that I was heading inside, I made a beeline for the gym. Mr. Smith was alone eating lunch. "Hey there," I started. "I sent Bobby in a few minutes ago to get a football for recess, and he said you wouldn't give him one. What's up?"

Mr. Smith's eyes got cold. "I told Bobby there would come a time when he'd need me for something, and he'd be out of luck. He's got to learn to behave."

To be fair to Mr. Smith, he was, in a stunningly inappropriate way, doing what he thought was right. He was following through on a consequence with the goal of helping Bobby learn to behave better. I wasn't appeased.

"Bobby's 8 years old!" I pushed. "You're modeling revenge to a 3rd grader? That's not a value I'm trying to teach my students! You're making him pay for a mistake he made a long time ago?"

"Mike," Mr. Smith said coldly, "that's why we have prisons in this country."

I was shocked. "Well, I'm taking a football to play with Bobby, and you need to know that you will never work with my students again."

When I got back to the playground, I apologized to Bobby. "I'm so sorry that happened to you, Bobby. Mr. Smith was wrong to do that. Let's throw the football around."

I wish I could say this was an isolated incident, but throughout my career, I've found myself having to protect vulnerable students from adults who are stuck in negative behavior patterns. One year, I had to stay in the classroom during our once-a-week recorder lesson when I found out that the recorder teacher was hammering Juan, a student she had developed a negative impression of. If I was in the room, the teacher was still dismissive and condescending, but she wasn't outright mean.

Once, I physically put myself between a colleague and a student during dismissal time near the buses. My colleague was upset and was yelling at a very small student, looming over him with a red face and pointing her finger right at his nose. It was scary. I stepped between them and told the child to head to their bus.

No doubt, instances like this can put us into conflict with colleagues, and that can be uncomfortable—even scary. But who else is going to protect your most vulnerable students? Very often, porcupines don't have parents who know how to advocate for them in school. School administrators can be unaware of unprofessional interactions your colleagues are having with students. You might be the only one who can step up and be the adult advocate that a struggling student needs.

Checking on Your Own Tone as Well

This is also a good time of year to check on your own tone and demeanor when it comes to interacting with your porcupines. A good friend and colleague of mine, Andy Dousis, wrote an article about how he realized he had slipped in his work with a porcupine (2007). In the middle of the year, he was shocked to hear some of his students mistreating Matthew, refusing to let him sit with them and dismissing him with impatience if he tried to work with them. He described how he had worked so hard in the beginning of the year to model kindness, inclusiveness, and patience and that his students had followed his lead. Matthew wasn't an easy kid to like. He often came to school dirty and disheveled with clothes that didn't fit. He struggled with academics and broke down sobbing easily. He pushed other kids and grabbed at their things.

So what happened mid-year? Andy reflected on his own interactions with Matthew and found his answer: He was tired and had let his patience slip. He was snapping at Matthew in frustration with a sharp edge to his tone of voice. He realized, "I wasn't just contributing to his mistreatment. I was teaching it. When I snapped at him, I gave permission to 23 others to snap at him too. I was using a surefire teaching strategy: modeling" (Dousis, 2007).

Teachers have so much power in the classroom. It's almost scary how much influence teachers have over the tone and tenor of their classes. Everyone gets tired, slips up, and says things they shouldn't. Your porcupines may wear you down, but when it happens, you can right the ship. You can get back on track and treat your porcupines with the respect that they need to be positive members of your class communities.

A Look Ahead: Navigating the Winter Doldrums

In the coming months, you'll need to work extra hard to provide awesome and engaging academic work for your students. Mid-to-late winter can be a time of incredible energy and productivity, but you can't just keep doing what you've been doing all year. If variety is the spice of life, get ready to spice things up to help navigate the winter doldrums.

The Winter Doldrums

February and March

All three 3rd grade classrooms at Sandown North Elementary School in Sandown, New Hampshire, were challenging. There were several porcupines in each room, and if students were bored, they got antsy and found other ways to keep themselves engaged—chatting with neighbors, wandering around the room, talking out, and more. It didn't take long for things to spiral. Discipline referrals were increasing.

Amy Difeo, the school's literacy coach, cooked up an idea to try (2024). She and the 3rd grade team decided to facilitate an independent inquiry unit on animals as part of a science unit on ecosystems. Each student would choose an animal to study, learn about their animal, and create some projects to share what they learned with each other.

There were clear curricular expectations, and each student had a checklist of the academic requirements to include. As the project progressed, the team collected data about engagement and on-task behavior and saw incredible increases in both. The school administration also noticed a dramatic decrease in discipline referrals during the project. The project culminated in a celebration of learning event where students shared their work with families and community members (Difeo, 2024).

When ships were powered mainly by wind, sailors dreaded getting caught in the doldrums. In areas near the equator, where the sun heats the air and warm air rises, there can be long periods near the surface of the earth with little or no wind. For days or even weeks, ships could be caught in these areas, making no forward progress as their food and supplies ran short.

You might expect late winter to be a time of great productivity and learning in school. The weather is crummy, and students are in good school shape. They know the routines, and you've started cool academic units. And sometimes, this is how it is. But there are other times when it feels like you're in the doldrums. Everyone is going through the motions, but you don't seem to be getting anywhere.

Cooking up a fun (and different) academic unit like Amy did is just one way to break up the winter doldrums. In this chapter, we'll explore a bunch of other ways to keep your porcupines (and all students) engaged. First, let's explore why this time of year can be so tough.

Avoiding the Third Quarter Slide

High school teachers know about the third quarter slide. Many high school kids struggle with stamina and motivation in mid-winter. Kids seem listless. They take bathroom breaks that last way too long. They struggle to get much done. And, of course, as is often the case, this phenomenon is especially pronounced in porcupines. There are a couple of factors that may lead kids to complacency during this time of year.

Grades Often Demotivate

If your school hasn't yet made the shift to competency-based grading, grades may be part of the problem. This might seem surprising, because grades are supposed to be what motivate students, but decades of research (Deci & Flaste, 1995; Kohn, 2018), not to mention my own experience, have shown the reverse to be true. For students who are taking a yearlong course and receive a grade for the full year, if they have a *D* or an *F*, they might rightly figure that they won't be able to get a good grade anyway, so why bother trying? Interestingly, kids with high grades can also suffer a grade-induced dip in motivation. They may figure that they have an *A* or a *B*, so they can coast a bit because they have a buffer. A few *C*s won't break the bank.

Motivation Drops After Midterms

If you've ever been an athlete, you know that motivation drops after a big event. You spend months training for a big race or the playoffs, and after it's over, you're tired, physically and emotionally. This is just what many kids experience after midterm exams. For schools whose calendars put midterms at the end of January, it's not uncommon to see kids take their foot off the gas pedal after exams are finished. They're cooked. They need a break.

There Are Colds and COVID and Flu, Oh My!

This time of year, respiratory viruses and stomach bugs rip through schools. Not only have friends and families gathered for the holidays, but in many places, the weather keeps people inside where it's easier to catch what everyone else has. It's not uncommon to go through stretches where 10–20 percent or more of students are out sick. I was recently talking with some high school teachers who support students who struggle academically. They talked about how overwhelmed some kids get when they return from school after missing a week. It's hard for them to have any stamina for work. They're still exhausted from being sick, and the amount of work to make up is daunting.

Navigating the Winter Doldrums

There are several ways you can combat the winter doldrums.

Ease into the Third Quarter

Make sure that the beginning of the third quarter is a soft landing. Instead of diving right into a complex project or intense lecture and note-taking sessions, consider watching a few videos to kick-start your next unit. Keep kids cognitively engaged by having periodic partner or small-group chats as they watch. Are there some simple games kids could play to introduce or review content? Could you read a story aloud? Also, can you back off on homework or out-of-class work for a few days while kids catch their breath?

Offer a Catch-Up Day

You might also consider having a catch-up day if lots of kids have been out sick. You could plan this as a whole school, or you could simply create one for your class of students. Have a day where there are no new assignments and instruction. It's a day for kids to work through things they're behind on. My son's university offered these occasionally. When professors noticed kids getting overwhelmed, the whole school would cancel class for a day so students could catch up. You could have a few fun activities ready for kids who don't need to catch up, such as a cool video to watch or some fun academic games to play. If you work with an individual student who has missed a lot of school due to illness, find a way to reduce their workload. Can you adjust a project so they can still be successful? Can you take a couple of assignments off their plates so they can focus on the assignments that are most important?

Rearrange the Furniture

Sometimes, giving your space a fresh look can bring more energy to the classroom. Have students generate ideas for how to rework the arrangement of tables and desks, and then spend a class period moving things around.

Add Something New to the Room

One year, I got a fish tank in my classroom in the middle of the year. This had nothing to do with our academic work, and I don't even remember how this ended up happening. What I do remember is how it changed the whole feel of the classroom. Students had something new to look at. The lights and sound of water flowing changed how the classroom felt. Consider what else you might add. Could you set up a puzzle table for when kids have a few minutes of downtime? How about a new bookshelf? Again, consider asking your students for ideas of ways you might liven things up a bit.

Remember to Get Students Moving

If you see heads nodding and kids yawning, it might be time for an energizer. Have students engage in a walk-and-talk partner chat about content, or have students engage in a short scavenger hunt for obtuse angles or words with the "ou" vowel combination around the room. Movement increases blood flow, which can increase physical and mental energy.

Work to Change Your Schedule for Next Year

If you happen to serve on a scheduling committee in your district, it might also be worth supporting a calendar change so that semesters end right before the holiday vacation. This would give students a natural break after exams, helping them start the second semester with fresh energy and enthusiasm.

Continuing to Build Positive Relationships

Relationship building is a yearlong endeavor. There might be some students who you're still trying to connect with because it's taking a long time for them to trust you. Or you might have good connections with some of your most challenging students, and you don't want to lose that. It's a bit like being in a healthy marriage. It takes work. If you start to take your relationship for granted and don't nurture it enough, your connection may fade.

Conduct a Schoolwide Relationship Audit

This is a great time of year to conduct a schoolwide relationship audit. Not all adults will be able to have a strong and positive relationship with every student, but just one strong connection with one adult can make a huge difference for a kid. Some schools conduct periodic relationship audits to see if any kids are falling through the cracks. Here's one way to structure such an audit.

1. Post all student names in a private space. Some schools use the teachers' lounge. Some use a different workspace where kids don't go. You could even use an online platform, as long as it's secure.

2. Have staff mark or note which students they have a positive connection with. This might be adding a sticky dot or writing a name next to students' names. Make sure to take time as a faculty to describe or define what this means (e.g., "You know this student well and have frequent positive interactions with them; they feel comfortable talking with you").

3. Look for students without connections. Hopefully there aren't many, but there are probably a few. Designate or assign adults who will work at building a positive relationship with each of these students. Make it a schoolwide goal that every kid has at least one meaningful connection with at least one adult.

Try the 2 × 10 Strategy

Each day, for 10 consecutive days, spend two minutes connecting with a student. Walk with them in the hall as you're traveling to the library. Chat before school starts or at the end of the day. Don't get too hung up on the exact numbers. The idea is to spend a little time each day for many days connecting.

This reminds me of parenting advice I once heard from a wise teacher. She tells parents to avoid trying to plan *quality time* with their children—instead focus on *quantity time*. Here's why. Let's say that you decide Saturday will be your family's quality time event. You're going to take your kids to the park. But then it rains. Or a kid is sick or grumpy. There's a lot of pressure on that trip to the park, and there are too many variables that might disrupt the time. Instead, she encourages parents to simply be with their kids . . . a lot. And then, quality often emerges during the quantity. You hang with your kid as they play with a LEGO set, and you end up having an unexpected deep conversation. You bring your kid to swim practice. Put your phone away and just watch them swim. You'll gain a new appreciation for how hard they work, and when they glance at the bleachers and see you watching them, they know you care. The same goes with your students. Time is precious, and students notice when you carve out time to simply be present with them.

Taking on a Challenging Academic Project

When students have met their psychological needs for autonomy, competence, purpose, belonging, curiosity, and fun, they can be highly motivated to do great academic work. Take a unit that's coming up and rework it to add some (or more) of these elements. It's amazing how a fun and challenging project can actually decrease dysregulation in students. I've seen this happen time and again.

Consider Many Possibilities

Research projects, such as the one highlighted at the beginning of this chapter, are one fun way to go, but there are so many more. Students could

- Create a class movie.
- Contribute pieces of writing to a class anthology that you could then publish and copy for all students.
- Create trading cards (based on sports cards or Magic cards). Students might describe characters from novels, create superheroes from the periodic table, or share about a historical figure. (There are so many possibilities here.)
- Dress up and pose as wax figures in a museum as part of a biography unit.
- Write and perform TED-style talks for each other or audiences about topics they're learning about.
- Create Minecraft versions of famous places or stop-motion animations of famous events.

The possibilities are limitless. If you're stumped and can't think of something awesome, ask your students. I'm sure they'll have some cool ideas.

Ensure Awesome Learning for All

It's important for all students to get to participate in these great learning events. These should not be reserved for "gifted and talented" students or kids who have finished assigned work first. Fun projects also shouldn't only be used as modifications to engage struggling learners. I've seen this happen. Two kids in a class struggle with motivation, so a teacher lets them do a fun and creative project—something that will capture their attention and keep them engaged—while the rest of the class does something more traditional and mundane. Instead, let all students do the fun and creative project.

Also make sure that whatever project you take on is something all students can engage in successfully: low-floor, high-ceiling activities. If students are conducting research projects, give topic choices, resource options, and project options that allow all kids to find appropriate challenge. If you're creating a class movie, have different roles and responsibilities so that all students can have a hand in the final production.

Staying Consistent with Discipline

It was mid-February, and I was working with a teacher who had a really rough group of students. One of her students got upset and in front of the whole class said, "I hate you. You're the worst teacher ever!" The teacher was on the verge of tears as she talked with me. "I didn't know what to do. I didn't know what to say. This isn't severe enough for her to be sent to the office, but it took all of my control not to cry in front of my class."

It's important to know what to do when these kinds of tough things happen. They fall in between a couple of spaces that are easier to navigate. For small stuff (kids swearing under their breath, calling out when they should raise their hand, etc.), simple reminders and redirections are enough. For big stuff (smashing a laptop, hitting a classmate, etc.), it's clear that kids need to be removed from the room and other adults, such as counselors or administrators, will get involved. But what about the in-between stuff—severe enough to be hurtful but not enough to warrant room removal?

Swearing at a classmate, calling the teacher a name, using a racial slur, and other inappropriate behaviors need clear, visible, and swift responses. This is important for a couple of reasons.

If Kids Think You Ignore a Behavior, They Think You Condone It

Imagine a group of students walking down the hall. One turns to another and says, "You've worn that sweatshirt three days in a row. What . . . are you too poor to buy a new one?" You hear the comment and so do the other kids nearby.

Early in my career, I probably would have pulled the student who said the mean comment aside for a stern talk, to protect their privacy and to not draw any more attention to the kid who was just insulted. I've realized, however, that this is a time to be public with a redirection.

If you ignore this comment, or even if kids think you ignore it, you may send the message to all the students—the one who said the mean comment, the victim, and the bystanders—that you're fine with it. Because teachers are the ultimate tone-setters in the classroom, this might then lead to these behaviors continuing or even escalating. That's why you need to act and to make sure your students know you're doing something.

Limits Create Safety, Which Improves Learning

Also, remember that some students are aggressive researchers. They need to know what the boundaries are. If, mid-year, you seem to stop holding students accountable for kind and respectful behavior, these students might wonder what happened to the boundaries. They may need to start testing limits again to figure out what the new limits are.

Then there are other students in the room who don't need to know what the limits are, but as they see disrespectful and unruly behavior go unchecked, they get unsettled—a bit dysregulated. They may laugh when a student does something inappropriate, or they may get a bit inappropriate themselves.

I'm speaking from personal experience here. I was a very easy student in elementary school—compliant, polite, and willing to do what teachers wanted. But in 5th grade, my class was out of control. There were a few scary students. The teacher was mean-spirited, and her only response to misbehavior was to threaten and yell. There were fistfights in the room, and during one of them, a student flipped the teacher's desk over. Another time, that same student punched the teacher in front of everyone. I was terrified, and I hated school that year. I compensated by being a bit obnoxious. I would make a warbling noise like a bird in the back of my throat that the teacher couldn't locate. She'd walk right by me as I smiled innocently. Another antic was one my friend Fred and I cooked up. I would fake a sneeze, and he would stand up on his chair with arms upraised and announce loudly, "And may God bless you, my son!" I remember after the last day of school standing with Fred at the front door of the school and yelling back inside as loud as we could before running for summer.

That year was terrible due to a few tough kids and a teacher who couldn't set limits to create safety, and even "easy" students like me engaged in inappropriate behaviors.

The Emotional State of Teachers Matters

And last, but certainly not least, there's another reason you need to set clear limits in the classroom: Your emotional health matters. When kids are defiant, rude, and disrespectful, it hurts. Even when you have empathy for kids who are struggling, it can still feel personal, even if you know deep down that it's not really about you.

When you don't know what to do, you feel incompetent on top of feeling personally injured. And when you feel incompetent, it's almost impossible not to burn out. Knowing how to respond when a kid is struggling can help you feel more competent and productive.

It's Not OK to Hate a Child

It was mid-winter, and I was working with a teacher who was worn down. A boy in her class had been a handful all year. He always seemed to be up out of his seat, distracting other kids, and defying her redirections. As we started talking about strategies for her to try, she sighed and said, "At this point, I just hate him." It was the dispassionate voice she used that concerned me the most. She wasn't lashing out in a moment of fear or anger. She was simply stating a fact.

Not too long after that, I was talking with a middle school principal about some of the challenging students in his school. His voice was tight with worry. "I'm trying to help a few of my teachers, but they see these kids as the enemy. They hate them."

In my home growing up, "hate" was not a word we were allowed to use. I couldn't say that I hated a classmate any more than I could use a swear word. It was too powerful. It simply wasn't all right to hate.

Consider that if you truly hate someone, you want to see them fail. You may wish for bad things to happen to them and secretly enjoy it when they struggle. You may be unwilling to help them when others do bad things to them.

By mid-to-late winter, you may be exhausted and frustrated with a student. You may be angry with a student or even afraid of them. You might acknowledge that they make you feel incompetent. These emotions all hurt. But for some of your kids, you are their only hope. You may be the one person who can stand up for them or help them. They need you to be your best self, even when they're at their worst. It is never OK to hate a child.

Trying Reactive Strategies

Now that we've covered a few reasons why it's essential to respond when a kid says or does something hurtful, let's consider how we might respond. I use the word "might" intentionally. The following suggestions can provide you with a starting point, but be careful not to resort to lockstep student- or situation-blind responses. "Three strikes and you're out" or "If A happens, you always do B" approaches may feel comforting for adults, but they don't give the flexibility that your porcupines need. While you might have a few go-to strategies to use in these situations, responses should take individual students' needs into account.

Let's also remember that reactive strategies are most effective when delivered calmly, without anger. We must work at being warm while we're being demanding. In *The Gifts of Imperfection*, Brené Brown (2020) encourages us (not just teachers, but everyone) to consider how accountability and compassion can go hand in hand. She acknowledges that it's easier to blame and shame than it is to follow through with consequences. "Wouldn't it be better if we could be kinder, but firmer? How would our lives be different if there were less blame and more accountability?" (p. 26). She adds, "Setting boundaries and holding people accountable is a lot more work than shaming and blaming. But it's also much more effective. Shaming and blaming without accountability is toxic to couples, families, organizations, and communities" (p. 27).

Take a Classroom Break

If a kid is dysregulated to the point where they've said something mean, to you or another student, but they're not so dysregulated they need to leave the room, you might have them take a break in the classroom.

In their inspiring and practical book, *Time Out: Abuses and Effective Uses*, Jane Nelsen and H. Stephen Glenn (1992) are clear that this practice is not part of the traditional rewards-and-punishments approach to discipline. Instead, it's a kind of logical consequence. If you're out of control, you need to chill out and get your control back. This might be a designated spot in the room that you use all year with all students. This can be especially appropriate in an elementary classroom. For older kids, you might simply say, "That was hurtful and doesn't fit with our class rules. Grab a book and find a quiet spot to chill out. I'll come talk with you once I've cooled off."

Find a Buddy Teacher

Sometimes it's helpful to have a nearby colleague who can take a student for a little while so that you (and the student) can calm down. Some years, depending on the students I had and whether or not anyone needed it, I had a reciprocal deal with a colleague. She'd take my students, and I'd take hers. We proactively established this plan early in the year with both of our classes. That way, students knew ahead of time how the system worked and knew to ignore a kid from another class if they came in to sit quietly or read a book on the side of the room.

If you have a student who is likely to refuse to go to the buddy teacher's classroom, it often works to have your colleague come get them. Your student might be less willing to get into a power struggle with your colleague next door who they don't know as well.

Take Away a Privilege

If a student is being rude or hurtful during a certain activity, they might lose the privilege of engaging in that activity for a short amount of time. For example, a student gets overly excited when playing a class game and shouts at you, "No fair! You suck! You wanted the other team to win!" The next time you play a game like that, preferably sometime soon, they don't get to play. This is another clear logical consequence. "You got overly excited and said something disrespectful the last time we played a game, so this time, you won't get to play. You can try again next time."

I used this logical consequence once with two boys who were rude and disruptive with a substitute teacher when I was out for a day. The whole class had struggled, but it was clear from the guest teacher's note and reports from other students that these two had been over the top. The next time I was going to be out for a day, I let them know that they wouldn't be allowed to be in the classroom. I had two different grade-level colleagues each take them for the day. They were really upset about this and pleaded, "No, please, Mr. A! We can do it. We'll be respectful!" I was empathetic and even sympathetic. I knew they felt bad. But I also wanted them to experience the consequence to get the full benefit of the learning. "I know you're upset, but that's what's going to happen. The next time I'm out for a meeting or the day, you can try again, and we'll see how it goes." When that next time rolled around, I met with each of the boys to check in about how they were going to stay in control and be respectful. They both did much better.

Hold Problem-Solving Conferences (Not Lectures)

Remember to leverage the power of problem-solving conferences (PSCs) from Chapter 9 when you have students getting into negative patterns of behavior. If kids are struggling with kindness, respect, or self-control during predictable times, plan and conduct a problem-solving conference to try to collaboratively come up with some strategies they can try.

Remember, though, that problem-solving conferences aren't about delivering scolding lectures. You aren't having a problem-solving conference if you're simply trying to deliver a lesson or to reprimand. If you're doing most of the talking, it's not a true PSC. Every now and then, these may have a time and a place. You might simply need to deliver a message: "Silas, I was hurt when you called me a name earlier. I deserve to be treated with respect."

Also know that lectures aren't consequences. Sometimes, other students may complain, "Silas is always saying mean things, and nothing ever happens!" If all you're doing, over and over again, is nagging and lecturing Silas but never following through on consequences, those other students are right.

Don't Force Apologies

You might want a student to apologize to you or to others when they have said or done something hurtful. Sincere apologies can help mend feelings. When someone has done something wrong to me and they give me a heartfelt apology, I feel a little better. I don't think, however, that forcing students to apologize is helpful, and it might even do damage.

Let's return to a previous example. Marie, a socially popular 7th grader from a financially stable family, says to Olivia, a classmate who's currently living at the nearby homeless shelter, "You've worn that sweatshirt three days in a row. What . . . are you too poor to buy a new one?"

Clearly, something needs to happen. In the moment, you should let Marie (and the other students who may have heard this comment) know in no uncertain terms that what she said isn't all right. "Marie! That's not OK. We have a class rule about respecting others, and that's disrespectful. You and I will have a chat about this when we get back to the room."

What's an appropriate consequence? Perhaps Marie shouldn't be allowed to travel unsupervised in the hallways for a few days. She's shown that she's not able to be respectful when given the freedom to travel on her own. She might lose that freedom for a bit. But is this enough? You ache for Olivia and may either want Marie to pay a steeper penalty (which may signal that you're really looking for a punishment) or want Marie to make it up to Olivia.

First, hold back on your longing for retribution. Punishments tend to backfire in the long run. Don't discount how uncomfortable it may be for a middle school student to lose the freedom of traveling in the halls without an adult. Second, what might happen if you try to force Marie to apologize to Olivia? No doubt, Olivia will know this is a forced apology and will likely feel further embarrassed and diminished. This won't make her feel better. Also, you have now taken some of Marie's power away. You've forced her to submit. She's likely to feel resentful. Might she decide to find a subtle way to take this out on Olivia—to get her power back? You may have just made things much worse for Olivia.

Instead, you might suggest to Marie that she apologize to Olivia if she's sorry. "Marie, if you were just upset in the moment and that comment came out, you probably feel pretty bad. You might want to apologize to Olivia. That might make you both feel a bit better."

Regardless of whether Marie apologizes to Olivia, you should probably pull Olivia aside for a quick private chat at some point. You might let her know that you feel awful about what happened and that Marie has lost the privilege of walking alone in the hallways for a while to make sure that Olivia is safe.

Model Apologizing When Appropriate

Everyone screws up. You may get emotional, say something you shouldn't, and know that you've hurt a kid's feelings. Or you impose a consequence and realize that it was too harsh.

I remember one time I was trying to help Darren learn responsibility. He was having a hard time remembering to bring in his safety patrol belt—the bright yellow strap that older kids use when helping younger kids with dismissal. We had a problem-solving conference in the late fall to come up with a plan, and we agreed that he would need to not forget his belt more than 10 times to go on the 5th grade field trip to a water park that was supposed to be the "payment" for being on safety patrol. (I didn't love this system, but as a first-year 5th grade teacher on this team, I needed to go along with it.) A few days before the big trip, Darren forgot his belt for the eleventh time. He was devastated, and my heart broke. He lived a few days a week with his mom and a few with his dad. He and his younger sister (who he often took care of) alternated weekends at parents' houses. His stuff was all over the place, and a safety patrol belt was easy to lose.

I went to the other 5th grade teachers and asked them how many of their students had also lost the field trip because of a lack of responsibility. One replied, "None. We just tell them they need to be responsible and threaten to take away the trip, but they always all go." I was furious, and I marched immediately to Darren. "Darren. I am so sorry. I didn't really understand how the field trip works. Forget about the deal we made. You're going on the field trip." We were both relieved.

Everyone is going to make mistakes. They give you the chance to model humility, vulnerability, and the strength to do what's right.

Celebrating Successes, Noticing Positives

Let's not lose sight of the importance of success as a motivator. You might have been really good at noticing and naming positive behaviors early in the year. Is that still happening, or do you find that most of your "management" talk is about reminding and redirecting? Kids have learned a lot at this point in the year. They've gained new skills. They've accomplished a lot. Is that being celebrated? Remember that competence is one of the most important intrinsic motivators. When kids know they're learning, growing, and being successful, they can continue to be motivated for new challenges.

Name Small Successes

As you're walking around the classroom and kids are working, name some of the small successes they're having as they work.

- "Phew! That was a tough word, but you nailed it!"
- "Yep, the answer to that problem is 27.13. You got it."
- To the class: "We just stayed focused and engaged in writing for 25 minutes straight. Wow. Congratulations! Let's celebrate with a quick game."
- "Jamie, I know you were frustrated with Joise just then, but you take a couple of breaths and stayed calm. That helped you be able to keep moving forward with your project!"

These small comments, woven throughout the day, set a positive tone in the classroom and let kids know that you're seeing their growth and progress.

Have Occasional Fun Celebrations

You might have wondered about the third example in the above list—where the class played a quick game as a celebration for a good work period. Isn't that a reward? Shouldn't we avoid incentivizing learning and behavior? This is a topic I dig into in *Tackling the Motivation Crisis* (2021). The cover has a picture of a pizza box, and the subtitle is *How to Activate Student Learning Without Behavior Charts, Pizza Parties, or Other Hard-to-Quit Incentive Systems*. But I hope people don't think I'm anti-pizza parties. I am totally pro-pizza parties. We should probably have more pizza (or other) parties in school.

You can have celebrations without using them as incentives. They're incentives if you dangle them ahead of time to motivate behavior. "If you work *really* hard this week, we'll have a celebration on Friday!" That's when rewards reduce students' autonomy (they have to do what you want to get what they want), diminish students' motivation for learning (the learning is the crummy thing they have to do to get the incentive), and signal a low opinion of students' character (teachers think students don't care about learning so they're bribing them). These are not your goals when you incentivize, but they're some unintended consequences.

If you have a celebration spontaneously, without having used it as a motivator, you don't tend to see these detrimental effects (Anderson, 2021). Throw a pizza party to celebrate the end of a science unit. Get up and play a fun game after students stay focused and engaged for a quiz. Be careful, though. If you offer a spontaneous celebration every Friday afternoon for three Fridays in a row, kids will start to see these celebrations as incentives. Students might ask, "If we work really hard during reading, will we get some extra recess?" You might chuckle and say, "No. That's just an every-now-and-then thing. We want to work hard in reading so we can get better at reading!"

Is WIN Working?

Many schools have incorporated a WIN (What I Need) block into their daily or weekly schedules. The idea is that this is a time dedicated to supporting kids' individual needs as learners. It could be a time for some learners to get extra one-on-one or small-group instruction. Some students may have time to catch up on unfinished work or to retake a quiz or test to demonstrate further learning. Other students might end up with an enrichment period—a chance to engage in extra or different learning opportunities. Although all students should theoretically benefit from a WIN block, these times are usually put in place with the neediest students in mind.

This is a great time of year to examine whether or not this block of time is working as intended. If not, are there tweaks you could put in place to make it better the rest of the year? Or is it time to have a bigger discussion about how WIN might be structured next year? If a major overhaul is needed, waiting until next fall rolls around will mean it's too late. Here are some questions to guide your thinking.

Are the Neediest Students Getting What They Need?

Again, ideally, this time benefits all students, but it had better be working for the kids it's specially designed for. Are students who need extra help getting it? Are they getting one-on-one or small-group instruction?

Are kids who are behind catching up? Are students who need to retake summative assessments doing so? If not, what are the barriers? Are there simple ways to remove those barriers?

Is the WIN Block Making Logistics More or Less Challenging?

The idea of having a dedicated WIN block is that teachers don't need to change their instruction or class periods. WIN is a time to get to the things that don't normally fit. Is that happening? Does WIN make the day or week feel more or less settled? Does it make teaching and learning easier or harder? If WIN is causing so many coordination and logistical challenges that it seems to be adding stress to the week, it may be hurting more than it's helping. Are there ways to streamline logistics to make things smoother?

What If Students Got What They Need Every Block of the Day?

Could it be that WIN blocks actually discourage differentiation in the classroom? Are there some teachers who, instead of offering differentiated learning efforts, figure, "It's all right if not everyone can get this right now because they can get help during WIN"? An alternative to a school-wide WIN block is to encourage all teachers to differentiate learning so that every lesson and assignment offers students reasonably challenging work (What They Need). Similarly, teachers can carve out smaller blocks of time each class period (especially if a school has block scheduling that allows for longer periods of time in each class) for students to get extra one-on-one or small-group support, retake quizzes, or catch up on missing work. This allows each teacher to structure WIN time into class periods as they see fit instead of having all teachers and classrooms use it whether it's needed or not.

A Look Ahead: The Beginning of the End Is Near

As winter winds down and spring emerges, students, and especially porcupines, may start to anticipate the end of the year. They may start to worry about leaving the comfort and safety of your class. They may worry about what school will be like next year. Will they be able to handle new academics? Who will be in their class? Will their teacher be nice?

It might seem like March is too early, but now's the perfect time to start to anticipate the end of the year. How will you help ease students' worries? How will you continue to build their sense of competence and connection with you and their classmates? That's what we'll dig into in the next chapter.

The Beginning of
the End of the Year

March and April

Things can accelerate this time of year, for better or worse. Let's start with worse.

You've heard about Allen before. He was the one who acted out pooping on the floor during a morning meeting. All year long was hard, and it came to a head in early spring. His behavior got worse. He started saying sexually explicit comments to girls during lunch, and several parents threatened to pull their children from our school if he had any further contact with them. It felt like every time my back was turned, he said something inappropriate to a classmate. He swore more, worked less, and fell apart more frequently. He was wearing down, and we needed to do something to save him from his actions while also making sure other kids could have a positive school experience. Although paperwork was in motion to get him more support, we needed a more immediate solution. The school ended up hiring a guest teacher (a more professional title than "substitute") to shadow him for the last couple of months of school. He needed someone with him all the time to help him stay in control. He couldn't eat lunch or play at recess with the rest of the grade, and she would accompany him to the bathroom, calling into the boys' room to make sure it was empty before he entered. My heart broke for him, but it was the best we could come up with to survive the rest of the year.

And now for the better.

It was early April, and I was in a scheduling committee meeting. I was out of my classroom for a whole day with a team of colleagues trying to put together our lunch and specials schedules for the following year. There was a guest teacher in my class—a young guy right out of college who was thinking of going into teaching but who had no real classroom experience.

One of the most challenging students of my career, Mark (the one who had been stabbing scissors into the carpet), had been to court the day before and was going to be removed from his home and placed in foster care. I had heard this was happening, but in the hubbub of preparing to be out of the room and getting things ready for a guest teacher, I had lost track of it.

At morning meeting, Mark asked to share news with the class. In a moment of incredible vulnerability, he shared, "I went to court last night, and I'm being taken away from my mom because we fight too much. I'm going to have foster parents, and I'm really scared. I'm ready for questions and comments." The guest teacher, stunned, had no idea what to do, so he simply watched as students' hands shot up to react to Mark's story. They were incredible and showed how far our classroom community had come that year. "Are you still going to come to our school? You're not leaving, are you?" "Have you met your foster parents yet? Where do they live?" "You must be really nervous."

Right after the morning meeting, Mark's school counselor came in to check in on him and took him down to the counseling office for a while. Tommy, another student in the class, called an impromptu meeting in a corner of the room with some other students. "Mark's in a tough place. We should make sure to take care of him today. Let's make sure he's never by himself." For the rest of the day, the class rallied. Kids invited him to sit with them at lunch. They asked him to play soccer at recess. The guest teacher shared that he always had someone by his side, sometimes leaning on his shoulder.

There's something about this time of year that seems to bring issues to a head. March starts to feel like the beginning of the end of the year. Some of your students will already begin to feel anxious about the transition to next year, even in late winter and early spring. You might start to see some behaviors that you thought were finished. Young children might break down in tears more easily. Older students might start to grumble about work or even shut down altogether more frequently. You might also start to feel some trepidation about the end of the year as you think of how much there still is to do. And everyone is so tired by early spring!

Let's consider some ideas for how to keep the ship steady during this challenging time of year.

Nurturing All Elements of the Three-Legged Stool

This is a good time to check the pulse of all three legs of your stool. How are relationships and community building going? What are some strengths and areas to work on? How about academics? Are students feeling supported and empowered? Do you have some awesome and engaging academic work coming up in the next few weeks? Are there any units that could use some improvements? And how about discipline and management? Are you continuing to be clear and consistent and warm and demanding?

Let's take a quick look at each of these legs before we move on to some more timely ideas to consider. Here are some reminders about ideas we've explored throughout this book.

Positive Relationships

Remember that students need connection and belonging with us and with their peers to be positively engaged in school. Are you working with a student who is still struggling to find connections with other kids? Could you pair them with a peer who you think they might get along with during an academic time? Could you invite students in for a lunch gathering and include students who might connect with your struggling student?

How about your own relationships with students? Have you had some tension lately with a student—perhaps you've been engaging in power struggles? Remember to not give up on kids! It's better to be in a complicated relationship than to be distant, so keep finding ways to be playful and connected in between the challenging episodes. Also remember to keep modeling respect for students, even when they're being disrespectful to you. I once heard a middle school teacher who said, "I'll give these kids some respect once they start showing me some respect!" That's expecting the wrong person to be the grown-up. They won't learn to handle frustration and anger with grace and compassion if they don't see what that looks like from others.

Engaging Academics

Keep paying attention to intrinsic motivators: competence, belonging, autonomy, purpose, curiosity, and fun. Remember that students can't be self-motivated without autonomy. What are some choices you could offer students with their work? Could some of those choices allow students to be more competent? Remember that it's awfully hard to keep working at something if you think you're bad at it. How can you give your porcupines some within-reach challenges? How can you empower them to work independently and give them a bit of support (but not so much that you're enabling)?

Make sure that your porcupines are fully included in the regular work of the classroom. If they're being pulled out of their regular class for small-group instruction, they may feel like they don't really belong in your class. How can you get more of the support work they need integrated into the regular work of the room?

Respectful Discipline

Make sure that most of your discipline and management work continues to be proactive. Keep talking about the classroom rules as the anchor of discipline in the classroom (look back at Figure 7.1 on p. 73 for a reminder). Set kids up for success with strategies such as modeling, proactive reminding, eliciting ideas from students, and the fishbowl. Remember that the more time you spend on positive and proactive discipline, the less you'll need to spend in reactive mode.

When you *are* in reactive mode, make sure to stay consistent, clear, direct, and respectful. When you're warm and demanding, kids feel safe and spend less time on the edge of fight, flight, or freeze. Remind and redirect firmly and without anger. Let consequences fall for small things. Keep honoring the rules of the class with action.

Starting to Talk About the Transition to Next Year

It might be tempting to shut down any talk about the end of the year. "We still have a long way to go. Don't start thinking about summer already!" You might worry that talking about the end of the year will only exacerbate students' worries. Might it not be better to pretend the end of the year isn't looming?

I don't think so. The transition at the end of the year is a big one, and it's going to take some students a lot of time to process that big change. You may also want to orchestrate closure at that time. I always wanted my students to feel a certain way about the end of the year. Here are a few qualities I wanted to nurture.

- **Excitement.** I wanted students to look forward to next year—to be excited about cool projects and interesting new content they were going to experience.

- **Pride.** I wanted students to feel proud of their growth and learning. They should recognize how much they have accomplished and feel ready for new challenges.
- **Nostalgia.** I wanted students to feel sad about leaving our class community. I wanted them to know that I was sad to see them move on.

What are some of the emotions you hope for students to feel about the transition to next year? Take some time now to think about and articulate those goals. Then you can start weaving in small comments about the end of the year to prime the pump. You shouldn't lay this on too thick. You certainly don't want kids feeling like the year is almost over with a few months to go. Instead, consider sliding in little comments here and there. After Billy does something goofy (again), you might sigh, smile, and turn to a nearby student: "What am I going to do next year without Billy around to make me chuckle?" As you're working on a math concept you might say, "This is something you'll take to the next level next year when you learn how to add and subtract fractions with unlike denominators." When you work with a student in a one-on-one academic conference you might say, "Wow, Julianne. You have come so far this year. There's no way you could have read that passage so smoothly a few months ago. Congratulations!"

Recognizing School Fatigue

School is tiring, and late winter and early spring can be times of extreme school fatigue. Kids have been going to school for months, and the last vacation may have been many weeks ago.

Cognitive Fatigue

Kids don't just get tired from school as the year wears on, however. They can get tired from mental exertion during a day or even class period. I was observing an 8th grade math class where kids were trying something new. Their teacher had given them four different choices for how to demonstrate competence: a traditional quiz, an online quiz, a fill-in-a-table option, and a set of problems of varying difficulties where they needed to choose the just-right problems to solve. Not only was the math exhausting, but making the choices was also tiring. Students also needed to write a short reflection after they completed their choices to share whether they thought they made a good choice. They worked so hard for the full 50-minute period, and at the end, they looked like they'd all just climbed a mountain. The teacher getting them the next period was going to have no idea how hard they just worked and how tired they were. They probably didn't need social studies next. They needed a snack and a nap.

As it turns out, there's a biological explanation for this kind of exhaustion. According to *The Economist* (2022), "cognitive work results in chemical changes in the brain, which present behaviorally as fatigue." The article goes on to explain that a chemical called glutamate builds up in the lateral prefrontal cortex, the region of the brain that supports cognitive control. As this chemical builds up, the brain works to rebalance and sends messages to rest and recover that present as fatigue. In their book, *Willpower*, Roy Baumeister and John Tierney (2011) explain in detail how people's willpower drops as they experience cognitive fatigue. It gets progressively harder to force themselves to do challenging things the more cognitive work they do.

Consider how much cognitive effort your students are making at any given time. Are they having to think really hard about an academic task? Are they also having to practice skills of collaboration and self-control as they work with others? If you see kids starting to physically melt down— to look like they've just run a road race—their brains probably need a rest and reset. Have them eat a healthy snack, get a drink of water, take a short walk, try some stretching, or take some deep breaths. Teach them how to recognize the symptoms of cognitive fatigue and a repertoire of strategies for getting their energy back.

SAT Exhaustion

If you teach high school, there's a particular type of school fatigue you may recognize in March. Don't forget how tiring and stressful SAT time can be for students. Sure, many of your students don't take it as seriously as you'd like. For those who do, they may be studying and preparing in the weeks leading up to the exam. Then, when they return to school right after the test, they may be a bit zombie-like. Keep this in mind as you consider students' workloads. You might ease off on homework and intense academic work in the weeks before and then a few days after SATs. Certainly, don't schedule tests or big projects to be finished right around this time.

Supporting Positive Energy

Here are a few ideas to help keep students' energy fresh even during a tough time of the school year.

Each Day Is a Fresh Start

Consider how it must feel to be a student who has to go back to school on Tuesday after having an epic meltdown or getting into a lot of trouble on Monday. They ride the bus to school worried about the coming day, dreading a repeat performance. They walk through the front doors, smiling and putting on a brave face, and they're greeted by a well-intentioned adult who says, with a pinched smile, "Good morning, Tracy! You're going to have a *good* day today, right?" There's an emphasis on the word good, and the meaning is clear. Yesterday is not forgotten, and you're already being watched.

Resist the urge to remind kids, even in a seemingly positive way, that you're anticipating more trouble and expecting better behavior. All these comments do is shove kids a bit closer to the fight, flight, or, freeze line, making them more, not less, likely to struggle. Instead, greet them like you greet everyone else—with a friendly smile and a "Good morning."

Continue to Use Respectful Discipline

As your school fatigue builds, be careful you don't slide back into the old habit of punishing and shaming students instead of using more effective and respectful consequences. There might be a part of you that is thinking, *I've been using logical consequences all year long, and this kid is still struggling. These just aren't working! Maybe I need to start using consequences that will really make a difference—like taking away lunch or recess or docking their grades.*

Consider this. If you have a student who is reading three grade levels lower than the grade they're in, would you expect that in the first half of the year you could coach, support, and give extra guidance, and they'll be all caught up by March? Of course not. Substantial academic growth takes time. It also takes a long time to develop better skills of emotional regulation and social interaction. If you think that consequences will teach kids impulse control strategies or get them to stop calling out in class, you've fallen back into the mindset of punishments.

Your students will likely need you to support them with natural and logical consequences all year long, and they'll need proactive teaching, support, and guidance to learn positive new strategies.

If you're getting frustrated with a student's behavior, instead of punishing them, write down a short list of skills or strategies that they're not using that might be helpful. Then teach them those strategies. For example, say that a student is still being disruptive during group work. Watch them and see what they're missing. Perhaps they don't know how to ask for a turn to share an idea, so they just interrupt and blurt. Maybe they don't really understand the task and are too embarrassed to ask. It could be that their group is shutting them out and they're justifiably mad. Once you've identified the need, you can do some teaching. Use modeling, eliciting ideas, a problem-solving conference, or other proactive strategies to give them the help they need. In this instance, you might also need to help the group be more inclusive and respectful.

Use Students' Names Positively

"Allen! Stop bothering that group!" "Allen, put that down!" "Allen, it's time to refocus and get to work." "Allen! We've already talked about this. You can have your phone back at the end of class!"

For some kids, their names can actually become an emotional trigger. I mentioned Allen earlier. He was the student who was so used to being in trouble and associated the use of his name with a reprimand, that simply hearing his name could set him off. I'd want to chat with him about his writing, and I'd call to him, "Hey, Allen," and he'd explode: "I wasn't doin' nothin'! Why is everybody picking on me!" Can you imagine how demoralizing it would be to have your heart sink or your hackles raise every time you heard your name?

One way to combat this is to make sure to use your porcupines' names in lots of positive contexts. "Hey, Allen, it's great to see you this morning!" "Allen, what'd you think of the Celtic's win last night?" "Allen, are those new sneakers?" "Allen, that was a really productive math period. Congratulations!"

Holding a Class Meeting to Support a Classmate

There may be times that you need to talk with your whole class about what's happening with a kid who's struggling, but you should do so cautiously and only when it's absolutely necessary. It's important to respect the privacy of students in crisis, and you don't want to make a tough situation worse. In my 15 years in the classroom, I did this once.

I got a phone call from a parent one evening. Brian's mom wanted to let me know that a classmate had said something troubling to Brian. Apparently, Jacob had told Brian "I'm going to stab you through the tongue with a knife and put a lock on it." When Brian told his mom this, he also let her know that Jacob had been saying disturbing things like this for a couple of weeks. I thanked her and let her know I'd follow up. I touched base with

Brian the next day and thanked him for letting his mom know what had happened. He let me know that Jacob had said weird things to other kids as well. As I started to check in with other kids, I realized this had been going on for a while, and it was serious. He had said scary things to many classmates, including saying to a student who was Jewish, "When I grow up, I'm going to be the next Hitler, and you'll be the first person I kill."

I told my principal what I had uncovered, and she had Jacob immediately removed from the classroom. He wasn't allowed back until she had had a meeting with him, his mother, his grandmother (who was the head of the household), and the school resource officer. I sent work down to the office, and he spent the next couple of days down there. With guidance from my principal and school counselor, I decided to have a class meeting about what had happened. Nearly all the other students knew what was going on already, so I decided I'd rather confront the issue directly, so everyone was on the same page.

There were two goals of the meeting. The first was to talk about the importance of being safe and telling adults when something scary is going on. I acknowledged that many of them had heard Jacob say some scary things, but that we weren't going to talk about those as a class. If kids wanted me to know something specific he'd said, they could tell me privately. I wanted to emphasize the importance of talking with trusted adults if they saw or heard something that was troubling. I got the sense that kids had been so warned about not tattling that they didn't tell adults when something serious was going on. It was important for my students to know that if Jacob said anything else that made them uncomfortable, they should tell me or another trusted adult right away.

The second goal was to talk about how we were going to help Jacob reenter the classroom when he returned. Not surprisingly, he was already struggling socially, and this wasn't helping any. As a class, we brainstormed ideas for how students could help him feel safe and welcome (while still taking care of themselves). We all agreed not to talk with him about what had happened unless he brought it up and to try to go about business as usual when he returned. Students said they'd make sure he was included in activities and would be kind and "normal" when working with him.

If you're going to try having a class meeting about something happening with a particular student, here are some questions to guide your thinking.

- Who should you check in with before you hold this meeting? Consider checking with an administrator, counselor, or a colleague. See if they have any advice about how to (or even whether to) have a class meeting about a student. See if they have any information or words of wisdom that can guide your thinking.

- What are your positive goals for this meeting? What do you hope to accomplish? Be crystal clear about this before you begin, and stay laser focused on your goals as the meeting unfolds.
- How will you protect the privacy of the student? Don't share more than you need to, and be ready to redirect a student who starts to share too much.
- How will you keep the meeting positive and productive? Don't let the meeting turn into a gripe-fest where students are venting about a classmate. Keep the tone of the meeting warm and demanding. You're here to support the class and help a struggling student, not to throw gas on the fire.

Keeping Your Classroom Neat and Organized

Back in Chapter 6, we considered some ways that the physical attributes of the classroom can play a role in engagement and behavior. The light and colors in a room can affect attention and mood. The arrangement of furniture can influence instruction and learning. Remember that these factors can especially affect students with ADHD and autism. This is a great time of year to reexamine the physical space of your classroom.

It's not unusual for classrooms to start to look tired by springtime. Posters look faded or have corners no longer secured to the walls. Materials and supplies are haphazardly strewn on back shelves and counters. *I meant to clean that up a couple of weeks ago. What happened?* Student work and anchor charts from units long since passed are still on display boards in the room or in the halls. If your classroom spaces look disheveled and disorganized, you might unintentionally send the message to students that you've given up. How can you demand good work and strong effort from students if you're surrounding them with signs that send the opposite message?

Here are a few things you might do to get your space back on track.

- **Take down old work.** If there are old projects still displayed on shelves or student posters from a unit that finished back in January still hanging on a display board, take them down. The same goes for anchor charts. If you have reminders and suggestions about persuasive writing still hanging, but you've long since moved on to another unit, take those down.

- **Display current work.** Send the message to your students that their work matters by having current student work displayed around the room and in hallways. Also display anchor charts and content displays that reflect current work.
- **Tidy up.** Pretend you've never been to your classroom before and look at your room with fresh eyes. Start in one corner of the room and slowly scan the space. What do you notice? Look for areas of clutter that can be cleaned up. Look for displays that are crooked or torn. Remember that a cluttered and disorganized classroom can be highly distracting for some students and sends a message to all students that you don't care about high-quality work.
- **Enlist students' help.** You don't need to do all this cleaning and reorganizing on your own. Have your students help. Invite student volunteers to join you for lunch to clean the room. Or take the last 10 minutes of a class period to straighten up. If your room needs more work, take a whole class period. Assign different tasks or areas of the room to small groups and get your classroom back in tip-top shape.

On Your Radar for Next Year: Healthy School Food

I was working in a school that serves a population living in extreme rural poverty. The school has been struggling with an overwhelming number of discipline issues over the last few years. They've had hundreds of discipline referrals, including ones for student-to-student violence. Many of their students are also chronically disengaged and exhausted.

After I had been observing the school for a couple of days, I met with the principal to share an idea. "What if there was something you could do here at the school that would increase students' attention for learning, increase students' abilities to self-regulate, assist with concentration and memory, decrease disruptive behaviors, and wouldn't require any change to any teachers' classroom practices?" The principal was intrigued.

What intervention could possibly offer such seemingly magical results? Healthy food.

Breakfast that morning was fried corn dogs, sugary apple sauce, and sugary apple juice. This isn't unusual. In most schools in which I work, I see the same kinds of breakfast foods served: pancakes, waffles, French toast sticks covered in sugar, sugary cereals, fruit "juice," and chocolate milk. Lunch is rarely better. Kids get pizza, chips, chocolate milk (again), nachos with processed cheese sauce, processed meats, and more fruit "juice" cocktails.

Kids get a burst of hard-to-control energy, and then they crash. They feel lethargic and grumpy and have a hard time attending or focusing. If I were planning a diet for kids to eat that would promote engaged learning and good behavior, this is the opposite of what I'd serve.

Also consider that for some students, especially those living in poverty, school provides most of their food for the day. For many kids, school breakfast and lunch are their only options, and some even get food to take home for the weekends. This was something we saw clearly during the COVID pandemic—many families count on school to feed their kids. Even wealthier suburban districts in some regions had school buses delivering school lunches to kids during lockdown.

This is something you probably can't do much about for the rest of this year. You'll need to work with your food services provider to think ahead. But it could well be worth it. A high school for kids with truancy and behavioral problems in Appleton, Wisconsin, was featured in the documentary *Super Size Me* in a segment about school lunches (Spurlock et al., 2004). They adopted a healthy lunch program that featured foods that were low in fat, low in sugar, free of dyes and preservatives, not fried, and not chemically processed. They didn't serve any beef. They served lots of whole grains, fresh fruits, and vegetables. They hand-prepared and baked most of their dishes. They also eliminated candy and soda machines throughout the school. They saw incredible changes. Behaviors were better. Kids were more focused in classrooms and were more productive with schoolwork. One administrator commented that if you walked the halls, the school didn't look like a school for kids with behavioral problems. They also pointed out that this program cost about the same as other school lunch programs.

This might seem like a big task to take on, but consider how much better off all your students (especially your porcupines!) might be if they had healthy foods to eat at school. Imagine if the foods they ate gave steady, long-lasting energy and fueled attention and stability.

A Look Ahead: The Last Weeks of School

Now the end is really in sight. It's time to think about how we want school to feel for kids in the last weeks of school. In Chapter 7, we considered how to be thoughtful and intentional about everything we did to help students transition into school in the first weeks. Now we'll think about how to devote that same kind of attention and care to the last weeks of school.

13

The Last Weeks of School

May and June

Mark was one of those students I thought about a lot—even after he had moved on to his next school (Anderson, 2015). He was challenging right from the start. I remember the very first day of school, when kids were heading to the bookshelves to pick out their first independent books of the year. He plunked himself down on the floor near the bookshelves, his face set in a hard scowl. I asked, "What's up, Mark?" He snarled, his blue eyes brimming with tears, "I can't read, and I hate school."

Reading was hard. Writing was hard. Math was hard. Lunch and recess were hard. Everything was hard. He crumpled work papers, fought on the playground, and teased other kids. It was even worse when I wasn't there. A substitute teacher once reported that he had been jumping off tables doing skateboarding moves. Several kids reported that he had etched "F**K" on the side of a bookshelf.

He came so far. By the end of the year, meltdowns were rare. He felt more confident as a student, and as I provided steady, firm, and kind guidance, he settled into himself and relaxed. He still often had a mischievous twinkle in his eye, but he was more likely to tell an appropriate joke or do something silly than he was to be hurtful or destructive. I looped with that class, and through much of the next year, Mark continued to make strong and positive progress. By March, he was practically reading on grade level. He was a responsible and trustworthy student, and he had lost his reputation with other school staff as a troublemaker. I knew he was ready for middle school.

And then came May, and it all fell apart.

He would explode, seemingly out of the blue—shouting in anger at me or a friend. He stopped bringing in homework. He put little effort into his work—even on year-end research projects that were motivational for others. Tears returned with a fury. Not only was I angry, but I was hurt. We had developed such a good rapport, and it was all going down in flames in the last weeks of school. I felt like a failure.

I sought advice from Gail, a mentor of mine across the hall. I described Mark's behaviors with frustration and annoyance, but her response shook me up. It wasn't what I was expecting: "He loves you," she stated. "He trusts you, he feels safe with you, and he's terrified to leave. You know, it's easier to leave mad than sad."

It's a bit like what often happens in families when high school seniors get grumpy and pick fights with their family the summer before they go to college—a phenomenon known as "soiling the nest." Have you seen this happen with some students? Sometimes the further the most troubled kids climb during the year, the further they fall at the end. This can be incredibly frustrating. After all, you pour your heart and soul into your porcupines. The ones who are the neediest are often the ones you attach to the most. To see them crumble at the end of the year can make you wonder if you accomplished anything at all.

Amid the craziness of the end of the year, it can be easy to lose sight of how scary this transition is for your neediest students. Many are about to begin summers with too little structure and safety. Many are terrified about what the next year will bring. And many love you and care about you, and they don't want to leave you. This can be especially acute for children who come from homes with lots of adult transitions and instability. For the past nine months, you have been the most, perhaps the only, stable adult in their lives.

As some students melt down over these next few weeks, remember to have empathy for them. They probably don't know why they are crashing, but they need your kindness, firmness, consistency, and love more than ever. They need you to be warm and demanding.

The end of the year may be the most stressful time of all. You panic about all you haven't covered. Schedules get wacky with end-of-year concerts, assemblies, guest speakers, and field trips. Many schools also have a lot of testing at the end of the year. Sports events and school plays and concerts run late into the evening, disrupting students' sleep. Many faculty start to feel like they have one foot in next year (writing IEPs, planning for placement, thinking about teaching new grades or courses) while still teaching their current students and managing their current responsibilities.

You'll probably start to notice evidence of kids' anxiety about the end of the year in small ways. Students start to nitpick at each other and feel more like siblings than classmates. Students may be emotionally fragile or struggle to stay engaged with work—seemingly running out of gas way before a period is finished. Little things may trigger big reactions: A bee buzzes in the room and everyone freaks out, or someone burps and no one can stop laughing.

The first weeks of school are important for building relationships, establishing routines, building academic excitement, and helping students ease into the new year. The last weeks of school are just as important. You can't (and probably shouldn't try to) eliminate all stress this time of year. But you also shouldn't just grit your teeth and hang on for dear life either. In this chapter, we'll explore some strategies for how to help students not just get through the last few weeks but also feel a sense of positive closure and eager anticipation for next year.

Being Warm and Demanding in the Last Weeks

It can be easy to be warm in late spring but not demanding. You might want to finish the year on a positive note and worry that if you're being a stickler for rules, kids will be upset and resent you. The finish line is in sight, and it's tempting to coast. You let little things slide and hesitate to follow through on consequences. Or you might swing the other way. You might be so stressed out that you let your anxiety about the end of the year spill over onto your students. Or you might just be run-down and tired, and it's hard to stay positive when mighty meltdowns ensue. But just like the rest of the year, your porcupines have the best shot at being stable and successful themselves if you stay balanced. Be clear, firm, and direct with expectations while also staying kind, understanding, and connected with your students.

Be Consistent with Routines

Many porcupines thrive on routines and struggle with flexibility. They get thrown when the schedule changes, and this is amplified in the last weeks of school. Whenever possible, hold onto routines to maintain some normalcy.

When my class took a field trip, I made sure that we all started the day sitting in the circle, just as we always did. We often didn't have time for a full morning meeting, but we would at least start with a simple greeting. Only a few of my students really needed this, but it was good for everyone. I was setting the tone: We're still in school, even though it's a different kind of day.

Think about the routines you have used all year long to support predictability and consistency. What can you keep doing, even when the schedule is different?

Kids this time of year will also need reminders about some things that were automatic just a few weeks ago, such as how to move through the hallways, how to follow expectations in the cafeteria or playground, and even how to raise their hands during class discussions. It might be easy to attribute this to some version of kids not caring. (*Now that the end is in sight, these kids just don't care about following rules anymore!*) It's likely that they're nervous and excited, preoccupied with the uncertainty of what comes next. It's easier to forget norms and routines, so all students—not just porcupines—will benefit from reminders.

Continue to Follow Through

Students also need you to continue to be firm and to follow through on expectations. This can be hard for you to do for the same reason it's hard for kids to remember them. You're preoccupied with the coming transition, and it takes energy and effort to hang tough.

You also need to be ready to redirect when kids get off track, and just like the rest of the year, the tone you use will determine whether you're being warm and demanding or just demanding. When you're feeling end-of-the-year stress, it's easier to slide into snark, blaming, or shaming. When your reminders and redirections take on that tone, kids who are already on the edge may slide right off. Porcupines need you to be kind and firm, now more than ever (Figure 13.1).

Continue to use natural and logical consequences to keep holding kids accountable for positive behavior and acceptable work. If kids are running up the slide, they should play somewhere else for the rest of recess. If a student leaves a mess at the end of a work period, they should clean it up. If they're not completing work and seem to be checking out of school, you should find a time for them to get caught up.

It is tempting in the last few weeks to start to let standards slide. You see a student speed-walking in the hall, and you're about to call them back to try again but then you figure—*Oh, it's almost the end of the year, I'll let it go.* Teachers let expectations slip at their peril. If you don't follow through on expectations, students will understand that you don't mean what you say or say what you mean. They will likely struggle even more to stay in control and further struggle with following expectations. Don't be surprised if behaviors start to spiral out of control.

FIGURE 13.1

Remind and Redirect

Instead of . . .	Why to Avoid	Try . . .
"Just because it's the end of the year, that doesn't give you an excuse to run in the hall!"	This implies that students are being wild on purpose and conveys low expectations.	"Remember to walk in the hall and keep your voices quiet."
"Do you think your teachers next year in 6th grade are going to put up with this nonsense?"	This sends the message that students aren't ready for next year, and their next year's teachers are ready to not like them.	"I know you're feeling nervous and excited right now. Try taking a few slow deep breaths to help yourself calm down."
"I'm so disappointed in your behavior. I thought you knew better than this."	This indicates that their behavior is ruining the relationship you've built.	"Stop. You're getting too loud. Mike, move to that seat over there."

Also remember that teacher–student relationships that are complicated (high in warmth, support, and conflict) are better than ones that are distant. If you stop holding kids accountable for good work and behavior, you're sending the message that you no longer care about them, and kids may further disengage.

Celebrating Accomplishments and Successes

It's hard for kids to see their own progress. Their growth is often so incremental. For students who struggle academically, they unfortunately likely feel unsuccessful a lot of the time. A sense of competence is one of the most important intrinsic motivators. If you can help students look forward to next year with a sense of accomplishment, they may feel more positive and energized about school next year. It's more motivating to build off successes than it is to try to improve weaknesses. Let's consider a few ideas for helping students finish the year with their heads held high.

- **Compare work samples.** Have students examine a piece of their work from early in the year and a current one. Have students identify ways their work has grown and improved over time. If you use portfolios, have students look back through their whole portfolio to identify evidence of growth.

- **Make a learning list.** You can do this with an individual student, a small group, or a whole class. Together, write a list of skills learned or topics covered over the course of the semester or year. Have students look back through notes, workbooks, or anthologies to gather ideas. Try doing this activity in several short sessions where students add new ideas to the list each session.

- **Write letters to next year's teachers.** First, have students make a list of several accomplishments they're proud of from the year. You might need to help students identify some of their most important learning. Then have students write a letter of introduction to next year's teachers. It might include a short introductory paragraph where they share some personal information and then a few short paragraphs sharing about their accomplishments. I strongly recommend that these letters be shared with next year's teachers. If it's done only as an academic task without follow though, students may rightly feel resentful.

- **Write letters to next year's students.** This is a similar idea to the last one, but instead of writing to their new teachers, they write to the students you'll have next year. They might share some student-to-student advice about how to be successful in this class. They can also share about learning projects and events that they thought were fun and interesting.

- **Create a time capsule.** This was something I tried with several classes, and it was an incredible bonding experience in the final weeks of school. Have students create or collect artifacts that highlight things they want to remember about the year. Although class jokes or funny moments are fine, make sure to get a lot of academic work in there too. Do you have pictures from the year to print? How about writing samples or small projects? You could even have students write notes or letters to their future selves. Put these things all in a box and set a date for a reunion. It might be a gathering after the summer or at the end of next year. It could even be further down the road. Several times, I had former 5th grade classes reunite at the end of 8th grade. One group had so much fun, they asked if we could put everything back in the time capsule and get back together after they graduated from high school. Eleven of them showed up, including one who could be pretty prickly back in 5th grade.

- **Create final fridge spaces.** Have students create a mini display highlighting a few proud moments from the year. What have they accomplished? How have they grown? What have they learned? Once these displays are finished, consider taking photos of each one to send to families.

- **Hold a spring celebration of learning.** You could take the above idea to a whole new level and host an informal open house for families in the final weeks of school. This might seem like a lot of work in the final weeks of the year, so if you try it, keep it low key with little to prepare on your part. Have students put together simple poster-style (or slide-style) displays highlighting learning and growth throughout the year. Invite families in for a final learning celebration. Families can roam, museum style, around the room as students share some of what they've learned. Just think about the pride and sense of accomplishment students might feel and how this would help everyone—students, families, and you—focus on positives as the year winds down.

There's an important side-benefit to carving out time at the end of the year for students to reflect on and celebrate their successes. It's good for you, too. Even as you worry about how your students will do next year, make sure to reflect on their (and your) successes. How have they grown this year? What can they do now that they couldn't do in the fall? Allow yourself to acknowledge the part you played in helping your students be successful.

Adjusting Expectations and Giving Students What They Need

As your porcupines in particular struggle in the last weeks of school, you may want to adjust expectations. This could involve an individual adjustment for a student or an adjustment for a whole class. One way to look at this is to ask yourself, "What do my students need right now, and how can I give that to them within the context of what we're learning?" You're likely feeling the impulse to cram as much teaching and learning as you can into these last few weeks, but if kids get overwhelmed and shut down, this doesn't do them any good. It's better to structure learning they can handle, even if it's a little less than you'd prefer. Students will learn more and be less dysregulated.

- **Shorten direct teaching.** A month or two ago, your students might have been able to hang in with you for a 15-minute whole-class lesson. Maybe now they can handle 10 or even 7 minutes. If you need more time for direct teaching, try splitting a lesson into two parts. Teach half of the lesson and give students a chance to apply or practice content. Then circle around for the second half of the lesson and give another chance for application and practice.

- **Shorten work periods.** Some students' stamina for work drops in the last few weeks. They're tired. In a middle or high school setting, you might divide a period (especially a longer block) into several shorter chunks to keep students active and engaged. In a self-contained elementary classroom, you might increase the number of learning blocks you have in a day. For example, 4th graders might need two 30-minute math periods instead of one 60-minute period.

- **Offer different learning experiences for individuals.** Remember the story from Chapter 9 about having Kelsey work with younger children in the afternoons? She fell apart nearly every day, so we gave her a different academic task that she could do. Is this ideal? Probably not. But it's better to have a student engaged in some learning rather than none. This might be another time of year to consider these kinds of ideas.

- **Build in more movement.** When students' energy is high, they may need more physical movement. You might offer more movement breaks—quick games or activities that give students a release, or you might build more movement into lessons themselves. It could even be as simple as having students stand for partner chats instead of staying in their seats. Remember to review expectations about these movement activities so students can be successful.

Keeping Learning Fun

A middle school science teacher shared a way he keeps learning moving forward in the last weeks of school. All the kids love the topic of outer space. It's a high-interest unit, so he saves it for last. His students are so excited that they can keep their focus and energy on learning even in the last days of school.

Of course, learning should be fun all year, but now it's more important than ever. Here are a few more ideas.

- **Offer students choices about learning.** Sometimes kids feel out of control at the end of the year. Schedules are wacky, and there's so much uncertainty about next year. Giving them even simple choices about academic work gives them some power and control. Keep in mind that too many choices can also overwhelm them this time of year. The choice between two sets of math problems to practice is probably better than five.

- **Play games to review content.** One way to keep things fun and reinforce key content is to play games about learning from the year. You might have students create question and answer cards to play a quiz type game like Jeopardy. Students could create simple board games with questions to answer. Keep these games light and relaxed. Deemphasize the competition portion, especially if you have some students who get too wound up when competing. Don't offer prizes or privileges to winners either, as this can make losing too emotional for some kids.

- **Extend learning students enjoy and can handle.** Are there certain learning activities that students especially love? Are there certain activities they can be successful with? Do more of these things, and reduce some of the activities you know they struggle with. I often found that independent reading and read-alouds were great end-of-year academics.

- **Try a mini research project.** This can be an especially fun way to stay productive in those few weeks after testing finishes. It can be hard for kids to focus on learning once AP tests or other spring assessments are over. Have students explore a topic of their choice that's connected with class content. They can spend a few days researching, put together a simple small project or two, and then share what they've learned with each other.

- **Introduce something new.** An art teacher I was working with recently said that she introduces clay as a material at the end of the year. It's different, so it piques students' interest. Consider introducing new materials like this at the end of the year. Or you might introduce a new learning activity that's high interest. Coordinate geometry was one of my favorites. Students love plotting points on graph paper to make their own connect-the-dots pictures.

Supporting Students with Spring Testing

As a kid, I remember loving standardized testing. I didn't understand why in Maine I was taking the Iowa test, but I didn't care. It was fun. I breezed through the math and literacy questions, feeling smart and accomplished. Most of the questions felt easy, and I was good at figuring out test questions. I was also good at focusing for long periods of time. Looking back now, I also recognize that because some of my classmates struggled with these tests, banging their fists on desks in frustration, I felt even better. I knew I was doing well relative to most of the rest of the class.

Your porcupines rarely feel this way about spring testing. Whether tests are standardized state-mandated ones or school or district assessments, these tests can be torture for kids who struggle in school. They may struggle with the academic content itself. The test questions are often poorly worded and confusing, even for kids with relatively good reading skills. Some kids might struggle with the skills of focus, attention, and frustration management often required to do well on standardized assessments. Add to this that many kids who struggle are often pulled out of their classrooms, away from their peers, to take these tests—a visible sign that they are different and need help—and you have a recipe for disaster for many kids. When considering intrinsic motivators, these tests make them feel in deficit on all fronts. Kids feel incompetent and lack belonging. They have no autonomy and little sense of purpose. The tests are rarely about topics they're curious about, and they're certainly not fun.

With all that in mind, let's consider a few ways to help porcupines get through spring testing.

- **Practice test questions.** If you write a morning message to students each day, you might include occasional questions about playful content that's structured like a standardized test question. For example, you might ask, "If you could only eat one breakfast food for a whole year, would you choose (a) eggs, (b) cereal, (c) waffles, or (d) none of the above?" This can help kids practice some of the language and formats of testing so it's more familiar.
- **Keep the rest of the day easy.** On testing days, don't have kids do any other heavy lifting. This is a great time to play some content-related videos, do some fun easy project work, or play some class games that review content from earlier in the year.
- **If students are being pulled for testing, see if they can invite a classmate.** It might be written into an IEP that a student needs to take tests in a small-group setting. If you have the space, could they invite along a classmate or two to join them? Or can you work it out so that lots of kids—not just kids who struggle—move into small-group settings? It might be a bit of a logistical challenge, but often testing time is all-hands-on-deck in a school anyway. If you've already got lots of adults helping with testing around the school, why

not have other kids join those small groups? It would probably help every porcupine better focus on testing, and it would help all kids feel like they're in it together.

- **Set a tone of calm focus and purpose.** If you talk about "getting through" testing or talk about how much you hate it, expect kids to have a sour attitude. Instead, you might say, "These tests help us as a school figure out what we're doing well and what we can still work on. Try to give a really good effort."

Supporting the Transition to Next Year

A fear of the unknown is what often seems to drive students, especially porcupines, into a distracted frenzy. *What will next year's classroom look like? What are next year's teachers like? Are they nice? What does the next school year's schedule look like? Can I be successful?* These are just some of the half-articulated questions swirling in their heads. The more you can help them envision next year, the better they can feel and the more they can relax at the end of this one.

Step-Up Day

Some elementary and K–8 schools devote time to stepping up to the next year. Current 1st graders go up to 2nd grade. Fifth graders move up to 6th. The top grade in the school has a special field trip to the next school they'll be attending.

If you structure this kind of event, make sure to have enough time for students to really visit with next year's teachers. Instead of just 5–10 minutes, try carving out time for students to do an activity with next year's teachers. If placement isn't fully decided yet, students might move by class to each of the teachers in the next year, spending time with each of them and playing simple get-to-know-each-other games. When you're meeting with next year's students, don't list lots of expectations or share too many details. This will just stress kids out. Instead, show that you're warm and supportive and talk about how you'll be demanding and empowering.

Here's a short example of what this might sound like:

We're going to do such fun and challenging work together next year! We're going to try some really fun projects. You'll get to construct hot air balloons as a math project (which we'll actually launch from the field) and learn about ecosystems through group research projects. We'll transform our classroom into world ecosystems! You're also going to get to read some great books and try some new kinds of writing. I'm especially excited to try a new writing unit next year—all about how to write fantasy stories. We'll learn a lot together in that unit. In order to do that great work, we're going to need to work together as a team, so when we get together in the fall, one of the first things we'll do is create classroom rules together. Those will give us all some guidelines about how we want our classroom to look and feel. Part of that work is having you all share some of your hopes and goals for next school year. That's something you can think about over the summer, if you want. What are some of your hopes for next year?

Teacher Visits

If students can't step up, can next year's teachers step down? You could invite each of the teachers in the next grade (again, this is especially for K–8 schools) to visit your students for some get-to-know-you chats. This shouldn't be about teachers listing what kids need to do to be ready for the next year. Instead, it's about getting to know the teachers. You might have your students prepare some questions ahead of time. "Do you have any pets?" "What are your favorite foods?" "Where did you grow up?" "What are some things you like about teaching 7th grade?"

If you're a teacher visiting a class, remember that the tone you set will be more important than any of the details you share. This is your next chance at a great first impression.

Video Introductions

In a middle or high school, where students will have many different teachers next year, all teaching faculty could create short (one- to two-minute) videos where they introduce themselves to kids and families. A simple template that everyone uses can help this feel less overwhelming and more consistent. For example, faculty all might share three personal pieces of information, two things they enjoy about teaching, and one fun fact from their own school experience. These videos can then be placed on the school's website (either public or password-protected). When students get their schedule for the following year, they can watch the videos to get acquainted with their new teachers.

Invite Former Students Back for Q&A

In the years I taught 5th grade in K–5 schools, the prospect of heading to middle school had many kids worried—especially ones without older siblings. Several times, I invited some of my former students to join my 5th graders for the last 30 minutes of a day in late spring. (This is easy logistically if schools are nearby and middle school dismisses early in the afternoon. If not, you might need to coordinate with teachers and parents.) My current 5th graders could ask my former 5th graders about 6th grade and the middle school. These sessions were fascinating. For some reason, my current students would always ask questions of 6th graders in this setting that they wouldn't during a step-up day. "Do kids really get shoved into lockers?" "What happens if you forget your locker combination?" (There were always questions about lockers.) "How much homework do you get?" "Is it true that you can get pizza every day for lunch?"

A Note About Summer Work and Fall Supplies

Some schools continue the practice of assigning summer work. High school students might be expected to read a novel and be ready to discuss it in the fall. Middle schoolers might be assigned the task of memorizing continents or countries in preparation for a social studies class. Elementary students are often encouraged to read books over the summer and to record these in a journal to be shared with next year's teacher. The practice of summer work is well-intentioned. You might be hoping to have kids' academics stay fresh to avoid the summer slide. You might want them to practice responsibility or to get a head start on next year's workload.

These practices can weigh on all students as they feel anxiety build around unmet expectations, but for some kids, the effects are more profound. And of course, porcupines often suffer the most. Not only do they not get the practice or head start you hoped for or the responsibility you hoped to build, but now they're starting off the new year feeling behind. The first day of school, they walk in already feeling incompetent.

There are other ways you might work toward some of your positive goals. Have a summer reading event where kids can come to read at school with teachers guiding discussions. Have a math party where there are a variety of math games to play with teachers facilitating the games. (If you're thinking that you like the idea of these things but you're worried teachers won't want to devote time in July to them, then you might also question why kids are expected to do schoolwork in the summer.)

You might also reconsider the practice that's still common in many schools of requiring students to bring supplies in the fall. I remember dropping over $200 one year for my two kids in middle school on three-ring binders, clear plastic sheets, markers, pens, a certain kind of calculator, and various other materials. You might teach in a school where most families can afford this, and back-to-school shopping might be a valued family tradition. But what happens to the kids whose family can't afford these things? They bring in used binders with torn covers and old calculators with buttons that don't always work from older siblings. Or they go to a special closet in the school with donated supplies. They use last year's markers instead of having fresh ones. The very kids you want to have a fresh and bright start to the new year feel diminished on their first day. If certain materials are required for students to have school success, make it a policy that the school must provide them.

These kinds of school traditions can be hard to shift. If you can't make the change for the coming year, perhaps you could open up the conversation for the following year.

Saying Goodbye

As much as you might look forward to the rest and relaxation that come with summer vacation, the end of the year can be emotionally tough. It's hard to say goodbye to students, especially ones you've poured so much of your mental and emotional energy into. It may be especially hard if they're out of control and pushing you away. I encourage you to think ahead about how you're going to say goodbye to your students, especially your porcupines, at the end of the year. You might write a short personal letter to each of your students to give to them on the last day of school. Recall a few of their successes, note a funny moment or two that you'll remember, and offer some encouragement about the coming year. Let them know that you care about them and that they can always come back to visit. I often wrote letters to students at the end of a year, and many parents let me know that their children kept these letters and read them over and over again. Instead of a letter, you could record a short goodbye video message and email it to each student on the last day.

There are many other possibilities. The key is to plan how you're going to say goodbye so that this doesn't get lost in the craziness and emotional whirlwind of the last few days of school. Also remember that your porcupines may feel overwhelmed during the last few days, even if they hide it well.

Mark, who I shared about at the beginning of this chapter, helped me understand that even though he was a train wreck in the last few weeks of school, he appreciated our time together. After that class walked out of the door, I sat in the back of my room and sobbed. It took me by surprise. I'm not much of a crier. But that class had been so hard—and so awesome. They were quirky and challenging, bright and mischievous, fun and infuriating. As I was calming down, I heard footsteps. I looked up, and Mark was coming back into the room. He'd ridden his bike partway home and then come back. He handed me a paper bag, said, "Thanks, Mr. A" with tears in his eyes and walked back out of the room. I opened the bag, and he had made me a "Certificate of Friendship and Teaching, awarded to Mr. Anderson" on his home computer and put it in a plastic frame. I put my head back down and cried a bit longer.

Conclusion

Hugging Porcupines Can Hurt—Do It Anyway

Sometimes we shy away from trying to build relationships with our most prickly students because we're worried about getting hurt. When we make overtures and a student lashes out, it's painful. We've probably all had students who have hurt our feelings, and that makes it hard for us to keep extending our care and love.

But this is exactly what our most challenging students need. They need us to show the absolute best example of what mature grown-up behavior can look like. They need us to not give up on them, even if they appear to have given up on themselves. They need us to model kindness amid turmoil and patience in the heart of chaos. How else will our most vulnerable students ever have a chance to exhibit patience, kindness, and unconditional love themselves if they don't have examples to look up to?

James

Remember James from Chapter 1? He was the student who faked asthma attacks to avoid writing and crashed his dad's pickup into another car. As I said earlier, he was one of those former students I kept thinking about over the years. I always wondered how he turned out. Out of the blue, many years after he was in my class in 5th grade, I got an email from him.

It was so wonderful to reconnect and hear how he was doing. He had graduated from high school, moved back across the country, taken some college courses, and settled into a new job, which he loved. He was also married and living comfortably. (He even sent me a picture of himself and his wife!) He reached out to let me know he was doing well and to thank me for not giving up on him years ago.

I've thought about his email a lot. James didn't talk about the geometric quilt that we created as a class math project. He didn't talk about reading and writing workshop. He didn't talk about our independent research projects in social studies. We did a lot of great academic work as a class that year, but that's not what James said was most important. "Stability, guidance, and care" were the attributes of our 5th grade class that James recalled. He talked about making friends and learning valuable life lessons. He didn't frame it quite this way, but he clearly appreciated being in a classroom that was warm and demanding and supportive and empowering. He ended the email by thanking me for changing his life that year.

If you've worked with kids for any significant amount of time, you've likely worked with one like James: tough, challenging, prickly, yet also caring and good hearted. James and I emailed back and forth several times, and in a subsequent email he expressed regret at how disruptive he had been and even said he had apologized to former classmates when he got the chance. He hadn't wanted to be so out of control. Of course he hadn't.

James's story is a great final reminder at the end of this book. As educators, we spend so much time worrying about curricula and content. We have standards and competencies to teach and assessments to administer. We know that many of the academic skills we are trying to teach are important for success in school and beyond. But for many kids, the academic content is perhaps the least important aspect of school. Are they safe? Are they building positive relationships with adults and peers? Are they learning how to understand and manage their emotions? Are they learning how to get along with others? These things, more than perhaps anything else, are what really matter for all students, but especially our porcupines.

So what if, instead of dreading getting some porcupines next year, you went to your administration and requested them?

Acknowledgments

It is with deep gratitude that I thank some of the many people who helped inform the writing of this book. First, thanks to the many educators who shared their stories, struggles, and successes with me. Your experiences have helped add richness and variety to this book. Thanks also to the many groups of teachers who heard excerpts of drafts of chapters and offered feedback.

There are also many colleagues who have offered advice along the way: Matthew Ebert, Sarah Edmunds, Jeffrey Benson, Erin Moore, Bryan Mascio, and Michael McSheehan. Your questions, support, ideas, and pushes added immeasurably to this work.

I also want to acknowledge and thank many of the educators who have informed my thinking over the years, especially when I was still in the classroom and learning how to better connect with, manage, and teach kids who have challenging behaviors. Marlynn Clayton, Ruth Charney, and Paula Denton helped me understand the importance of proactive teaching, having empathy for kids who struggle in school, and how to bring these understandings into practice. Your workshops, books, coaching, and direct mentorship helped shape me as an educator and a person. The work of Jim Fay and Foster Cline helped me understand how to let consequences fall without anger and how to keep my sense of humor when things get tough. I have also been inspired and informed by Ross Greene, whose work continues to protect and support kids around the world.

Finally, I'd like to thank Genny Ostertag, Liz Wegner, and the ISTE+ASCD team who have supported me and my writing for years. Your patience, insights, integrity, professionalism, and high standards helped keep this book manageable and clear. I continue to value our ongoing work together.

References

Anderson, M. (2015, May 15). Mighty meltdowns in the month of May. *Leading Great Learning*. https://leadinggreatlearning.com/mighty-meltdowns-in-the-month-of-may/

Anderson, M. (2016a, October 3). How well do you know your students? *Leading Great Learning*. https://leadinggreatlearning.com/how-well-do-you-know-your-students/

Anderson, M. (2016b, December 31). 12 routines to revisit in January. *Leading Great Learning*. https://leadinggreatlearning.com/revisiting-routines-in-january/

Anderson, M. (2018). Getting consistent with consequences. *Educational Leadership, 76*(1). https://www.ascd.org/el/articles/getting-consistent-with-consequences

Anderson, M. (2019, September 2). Hugging porcupines: Building meaningful relationships with our toughest students. *Leading Great Learning*. https://leadinggreatlearning.com/hugging-porcupines-building-meaningful-relationships-with-our-toughest-students/

Anderson, M. (2021). *Tackling the motivation crisis: How to activate student learning without behavior charts, pizza parties, or other hard-to-quit incentive systems*. ASCD.

Baker, J. A. (2006). Contributions of teacher–child relationships to positive school adjustment during elementary school. *Journal of School Psychology, 44*(3), 211–229.

Baumeister, R. F., & Tierney, J. (2011). *Willpower: Rediscovering the greatest human strength*. Penguin.

BBC. (2016, April 17). 'Boaty McBoatface' tops public vote as name of polar ship. https://www.bbc.com/news/uk-england-36064659

Benson, J. (2014). *Hanging in: Strategies for teaching the students who challenge us most*. ASCD.

Benson, J. (2015). How not to be a mountain troll. *Educational Leadership, 73*(2), 42–45. https://www.ascd.org/el/articles/how-not-to-be-a-mountain-troll

Benson, J. (2021). Online course: Hugging porcupines: Build positive relationships with kids who have challenging behaviors. https://courses.leadinggreatlearning.com/courses/hugging-porcupines

Brady, K., Forton, M. B., & Porter, D. (2011). *Rules in school: Teaching discipline in the responsive classroom* (2nd ed.). Northeast Foundation for Children.

Brooks, D. (2023). *How to know a person: The art of seeing others deeply and being deeply seen*. Random House.

Brown, B. (2020). *The gifts of imperfection*. Hazelden.

Budge, K. M., & Parrett, W. H. (2018). *Disrupting poverty: Five powerful classroom practices*. ASCD.

Burchinal, M. R., Peisner-Feinberg, E., Pianta, R., & Howes, C. (2002). Development of academic skills from preschool through second grade: Family and classroom predictors of developmental trajectories. *Journal of School Psychology, 40*(5), 415–436.

Burns, E. C., Van Bergen, P., Leonard, A., & Amin, Y. (2022). Positive, complicated, distant, and negative: How different teacher-student relationship profiles relate to students' science motivation. *Journal of Adolescence, 94*(8), 1150–1162.

Buyse, E., Verschueren, K., Doumen, S., Van Damme, J., & Maes, F. (2008). Classroom problem behavior and teacher-child relationships in kindergarten: The moderating role of classroom climate. *Journal of School Psychology, 46*(4), 367–391.

CDC. https://www.cdc.gov/child-development/resources/index.html

Charney, R. (2002). *Teaching children to care: Classroom management for ethical and academic growth, K–8*. Northeast Foundation for Children.

Deci, E., with Flaste, R. (1995). *Why we do what we do: Understanding self-motivation*. Penguin.

Deci, E., Koestner, R., & Ryan, R. (1999). A meta-analytic review of experiments examining the effects of extrinsic rewards on intrinsic motivation. *Psychological Bulletin, 125*(6), 627–668.

de Saint-Exupery, A. (1943). *The little prince*. Clarion Books.

Difeo, A. (2024, June 11). Struggling with motivation? Try engaging students with project-based learning! *Leading Great Learning*. https://leadinggreatlearning.com/struggling-with -motivation-try-engaging-students-with-project-based-learning/

Di Lisio, G., Halty, A., Berástegui, A., Milá Roa, A., & Couso Losada, A. (2025). The longitudinal associations between teacher-student relationships and school outcomes in typical and vulnerable student populations: A systematic review. *Social Psychology of Education, 28*(1), 144.

Dousis, A. (2007, April 1). What teaching Matthew taught me. *Responsive Classroom*. https:// www.responsiveclassroom.org/what-teaching-matthew-taught-me/

The Economist. (2022, August 11). How thinking hard makes the brain tired. https://www .economist.com/science-and-technology/2022/08/11/how-thinking-hard-makes-the -brain-tired

Emslander, V., Holzberger, D., Ofstad, S. B., Fischbach, A., & Scherer, R. (2025). Teacher-student relationships and student outcomes: A systematic second-order meta-analytic review. *Psychological Bulletin, 151*(3), 365–397.

Erwin, J. C. (2024). *The classroom of choice: 100+ strategies to reach and teach every learner* (2nd ed.). ASCD.

Furrer, C., & Skinner, E. (2003). Sense of relatedness as a factor in children's academic engagement and performance. *Journal of Educational Psychology, 95*(1), 148–162.

Gaines, K., & Curry, Z. (2011). The inclusive classroom: The effects of color on learning and behavior. *Journal of Family and Consumer Sciences Education, 29*(1).

Gehlbach, H., Brinkworth, M. E., King, A. M., Hsu, L. M., McIntyre, J., & Rogers, T. (2016). Creating birds of similar feathers: Leveraging similarity to improve teacher–student relationships and academic achievement. *Journal of Educational Psychology, 108*(3), 342–352.

Godwin, K. E., Leroux, A. J., Scupelli, P., & Fisher, A. V. (2022). Classroom design and children's attention allocation: Beyond the laboratory and into the classroom. *Mind, Brain, and Education, 16*(3), 239–251.

Greene, R. W. (1999). *The explosive child*. HarperCollins World.

Greene-Santos, A. (2024, May 20). Corporal punishment in schools still legal in many states. *NEA Today*. https://www.nea.org/nea-today/all-news-articles/corporal-punishment-schools-still -legal-many-states

Gregory, A., & Ripski, M. B. (2008). Adolescent trust in teachers: Implications for behavior in the high school classroom. *School Psychology Review, 37*(3), 337–353.

Gruman, D. H., Harachi, T. W., Abbott, R. D., Catalano, R. F., & Fleming, C. B. (2008). Longitudinal effects of student mobility on three dimensions of elementary school engagement. *Child Development, 79*(6), 1833–1852.

Haidt, J. (2024). *The anxious generation: How the great rewiring of childhood is causing an epidemic of mental illness*. Penguin.

Hamre, B. K., & Pianta, R. C. (2001). Early teacher–child relationships and the trajectory of children's school outcomes through eighth grade. *Child Development, 72*(2), 625–638.

Hattie, J. (2009). *Visible learning: A synthesis of over 800 meta-analyses relating to achievement*. Routledge.

Hume, K. (2007). Clean up your act! Creating an organized classroom environment for students on the spectrum. *The Reporter, 13*(1), 15–18.

King, R. B. (2015). Sense of relatedness boosts engagement, achievement, and well-being: A latent growth model study. *Contemporary Educational Psychology, 42*, 26–38.

Kleinfeld, J. (1975). Effective teachers of Eskimo and Indian students. *School Review, 83*, 301–344.

Kochanowicz, C. (2023, May 2). Can retakes actually raise the bar? *Leading Great Learning.* https://leadinggreatlearning.com/can-retakes-actually-raise-the-bar/

Kohn, A. (2018). *Punished by rewards: The trouble with gold stars, incentive plans, A's and praise* (25th anniversary edition). Mariner.

Liljedahl, P. (2021). *Building thinking classrooms in mathematics, grades K–12: 14 teaching practices for enhancing learning*. Corwin.

Mackenzie, R. J. (2013). *Setting limits with your strong-willed child: Eliminating conflict by establishing clear, firm, and respectful boundaries* (2nd ed.). Harmony.

Maslow, A. H. (1943). A theory of human motivation. *Psychological Review, 50*(4), 370–396.

Nelsen, J. (2006). *Positive discipline*. Ballentine Books.

Nelsen, J., & Glenn, H. S. (1992). *Time out: Abuses and effective uses*. Sunrise.

Pierson, R. (2013, May). Every kid needs a champion [Video]. TED. https://www.ted.com/talks/rita_pierson_every_kid_needs_a_champion

Rohr, J. (2022, September). A powerful proactive strategy: Positive phone calls to families. *Leading Great Learning.* https://leadinggreatlearning.com/a-powerful-proactive-strategy-positive-phone-calls-to-families/

Roorda, D. L., Koomen, H. M., Spilt, J. L., & Oort, F. J. (2011). The influence of affective teacher–student relationships on students' school engagement and achievement: A meta-analytic approach. *Review of Educational Research, 81*(4), 493–529.

Sachar, L. (1998). *Holes*. Farrar, Straus and Giroux.

Sanders, M. J. (2013). Classroom design and student engagement. *Proceedings of the Human Factors and Ergonomics Society Annual Meeting, 57*(1), 496–500. https://doi.org/10.1177/1541931213571107

Shalaby, C. (2017). *Troublemakers: Lessons in freedom from young children at school*. The New Press.

Souers, K., with Hall, P. (2016). *Fostering resilient learners: Strategies for creating a trauma-sensitive classroom*. ASCD.

Spurlock, M., Isaacs, D., Bennett, B., Ganjhu, L., Jamieson, A., Siegel, S., Horowitz, S., Parrish, M., & Ray, D. (2004). *Super size me*. Columbia TriStar Home Entertainment.

Stewart, T. E. (2007). *The mysterious benedict society*. Little Brown and Co., NY.

Venables, D. R. (2020). Five inconvenient truths about how we grade. *Educational Leadership, 78*(1). https://www.ascd.org/el/articles/five-inconvenient-truths-about-how-we-grade

Wood, C. (2017). *Yardsticks: Child and adolescent development ages 4–14* (4th ed.). Center for Responsive Schools.

Yuen, H. K., Wood, A. L., Krentel, J. E., Oster, R. A., Cunningham, A. D., & Jenkins, G. R. (2023). Emotional responses of college students to filtered fluorescent lighting in a classroom (v3). *Health Psychology Research, 11*.

Index

About the Author

 **Mike Anderson** has been an educator for many years. His first and primary love was as a public school classroom teacher, but he has had many other roles as well. He has coached swim teams, worked in preschools, taught university graduate-level classes, and worked as a consultant and developer for an educational nonprofit organization. In 2004, Anderson was awarded a national Milken Educator Award, and in 2005, he was a finalist for New Hampshire Teacher of the Year.

Now an independent education consultant, Anderson works with schools in rural, urban, and suburban settings across the United States and beyond. Anderson supports teachers and schools on the intersection of student engagement, positive relationships, and effective discipline. It is his firm belief that professional learning should be engaging and joyful and should model what great classroom teaching is all about. In 2020, he was awarded the Outstanding Educational Leader Award by NHASCD for his work as a consultant.

Anderson is the author of many books about great teaching and learning. To learn more about Anderson and his work, visit his website: www.leadinggreatlearning.com. Through that site you can read his blog, subscribe to his newsletter, connect with him on social media, and learn about the many online courses he has created for teachers.